CONTENTS

Introduction

LETTING PROPERTY FOR PROFIT

SEAN ANDREWS

Straightforward Guides

978-1-84716-779-8

Series Editor Roger Sproston

Printed by 4edge www.4edge.co.uk

Cover design by Bookworks Islington

Appendix 1
Useful Tips for a landlord

Appendix 2
Sample tenancy agreements and notices England, Wales and Scotland

****

INTRODUCTION

This revised edition of Letting Property for Profit has been expanded to cover Changes in the law to **2018**. Its aim is to demonstrate in a clear and uncomplicated way the key elements in buying and managing residential property. In the main the book is intended for the investor but can also be used by those who wish to gain a background in property management generally.

Although it is harder for the would be landlord to gain access to the buy-to-let sector at this point In time, the opportunities for landlords to invest and make a decent return are still there with more individuals and families moving into the private rented sector due to the ongoing rises in property prices. Overall, private letting of residential property has grown significantly in the last 30 years, However, in some cases those who are involved in letting property do not have the professional knowledge needed to manage effectively and often end up in a mess. Little thought is given to the fact that a complex framework of law, which both parties should recognise, covers the landlord and tenant, defining the relationship between the two.

Whilst the public sector has taken great pains to educate the landlord and tenant, the private sector has not followed suit. As a result, the government is giving increasing powers to local authorities to crack down on poor landlords. This is an inevitable consequence of the growth in private landlordism. This book should, hopefully remedy some of those shortcomings and make the process of managing property for a profit that much easier and also staying on the side of the law.

Introduction

Generally the key to understanding any situation is having knowledge of a particular subject. The law and business environment relating to housing is one very important area.

This Guide is intended to provide clear answers for the landlord, existing or potential by outlining the business and legal environment and also rights and obligations in general and by pointing to the way forward in a particular situation. The book covers the acquisition, letting and managing of property in depth and should enable the landlord, or potential landlord to manage effectively and efficiently, at the same time protecting his or her asset.

Also included in this revised edition is an updated detailed guide to landlord tax obligations (which have changed in the last few years, to the detriment of the private landlord) including capital gains tax and advice on how to minimize liability.

The guide should also be of use to the student who wants a brief introduction to the law relating to private residential lettings.

This book is essential reading for any landlord or potential landlord and should prove to be invaluable.

Sean Andrews

****

CHAPTER 1

Considerations When Renting Out a Property

....

Investing in Property generally

If finance can be arranged then the yields that one can expect from buy-to-let properties are high by comparison, currently standing at an average of 6%. However, it should be noted that yields will vary significantly depending on where you invest. For example, buying a property, and subsequent yields, will be a different matter in the south east by comparison to the north east.

A yield is a portfolio's annual rental income as a percentage of total value. The reason is that demand for private rented property is high, particularly as first time buyers cannot get a toehold in the market. They are instead turning to the private rental sector. Therefore, investing in property, for the longer term, as opposed to investing for short-term gain, is still a viable option.

As with everything, property is a good investment as long as it is managed well. Too many landlords (so called landlords) buy property and neglect it which has a negative impact on the environment and also a negative impact on the investment as a whole. A run down property will decrease in value and the possibility of renting it out for a full market rent will also diminish. That is what this book is all about-how to become a good landlord and a good property manager and how to maximize the returns on your property.

It should be noted that the Government, in 2018, is pushing for greater regulation for private sector properties let to private tenants and are giving local authorities more control over standards and are also pushing for longer tenancies to provide greater security for private tenants. Many local authorities will be introducing a licensing system for private landlords, in addition to the one in existence for Houses in Multiple Occupation.

The importance of having a clear business plan

Letting residential property for profit has become more and more common in the last thirty years, particularly since the passage of the 1988 Housing Act, which gave potential landlords more incentive to let by removing rent controls for property let after 1988 and also changing the tenancy in use to the assured tenancy, a version of which is the assured shorthold, fixed for a minimum period of six months and (relatively) easily ended after that period.

Added to the passage of the 1988 Act has been the activities of the housing market which boomed in the eighties and then predictably went bust, boomed again in the nineties and then went bust and then boomed again.

In addition to the many who let property out of necessity and who are not "professional landlords" so to speak, there are those who have built a business through acquiring properties, mostly through mortgage and letting them out for a profit. These professional landlords differ as to their expertise, some being very unprofessional in their approach, having no real idea of Landlord and Tenant law and no idea of the property world and subsequently very little idea of management. Often these people come unstuck and cause grief to others, whether intentionally or otherwise.

The aim of this section is to introduce the landlord, whether potential or already involved in the business, to the key aspects of the world of residential letting in the hope that that person becomes more knowledgeable and that profit is maximized whilst management is effective and equitable.

What kind of property is suitable for letting?

Obviously there are a number of different markets when it comes to people who rent. There are those who are less affluent, young and single, in need of a sharing situation, but more likely to require more intensive management than older more mature (perhaps professional) people who can afford a higher rent but require more for their money. The type of property you have, its location, its condition, will very much determine the rent levels that you can charge and the clients that you will attract.

The type of rent that a landlord might expect to achieve will be around ten per cent of the value of the freehold of the property, (or long leasehold in the case of flats). The eventual profit will be determined by the level of any existing mortgage and other outgoings.

If you are renting a flat it could be that it is in a mansion block or other flatted block and the service charge will need to be added to the rent. When letting a property for a profit it is necessary to consider profit after mortgage payments and likely tax bill plus other outgoings such as insurance and agents fees (if any). Of course there are other factors which make the profit achieved less important, that is the capital growth of the property. See further on in the book for a breakdown of taxation and allowances.

The business plan

As a (would be) private landlord, a person considering letting a property for profit, or already doing so, it is vital that you are very clear about the following:

- What kind of approach do you intend to take as a landlord? Do you intend to purchase, or do you have, an up market property which you are going to rent out to stable professional tenants who will pay their rent on time and look after the property (hopefully!).

- What are the key factors that affect the value of a property in rental terms? Is the property close to public transport, does it have a garden, what floor is it on and what size are the rooms? Is it secure and in a crime free area? If you are acquiring a property you should set out what it is you are trying to achieve in the longer term, i.e. the type of person you want and match this to the likely residential requirements of that hypothetical person. You can then gain an idea of what type of property you are looking for, in what area, and you can then see whether or not you can afford such a property. If not, you may have to change your plan.

- Do you intend to let to young single people, perhaps students, who will occupy individual rooms achieving higher returns but causing potentially greater headaches? Are you aware of the headaches? It is vitally important that you understand the ramifications of letting to different client groups and the potential problems in the future.

14

- Are you clear about the impact on the environment, and to other people, that your activities as a landlord may have? For example, do you have a maintenance plan which ensures that not only does your property look nice and remain well maintained but also takes into account whether the plan, or lack of it, will have an impact on the rest of the neighborhood? Will the type of tenant you intend to attract affect the rest of those living in the immediate vicinity

- What are the aims and objectives underpinning your business plan? Do you have a business plan or are you operating in an unstructured way? Taking into account the above, it is obviously necessary that you have a clear picture of the business environment that you intend to operate in and the legal and economic framework that governs and regulates the environment.

- It is vital that you are very clear about what it is you are trying to achieve. You should either understand the type of property that you already own or have an idea of the property you are trying to acquire to fit what client group. These goals should be very clear in your own mind and based on a long-term projection, underpinned by knowledge of the law and economics of letting property.

- As an exercise you should sit down and map out your business plan, before you go any further. Whether you are an existing property owner, or wish to acquire a property for the purpose of letting, the first objective is to formulate a business plan.

****

Chapter 2

Buying a House or Flat for Investment

....

Budget

Before beginning to look for a house or flat for investment you need to sit down and give careful thought to the costs.

Deposit

Sometimes the estate agent (if you are buying through an estate agent) will ask you for a small deposit when you make the offer. This indicates that you are serious about the offer and is a widespread and legitimate practice, as long as the deposit is not too much. £100 is usual.

The main deposit for the property, i.e. the difference between the mortgage and what has been accepted for the property, isn't paid until the exchange of contracts. Once you have exchanged contracts on a property the purchase is legally binding. Until then, you are free to withdraw. The deposit cannot be reclaimed after exchange.

Banks will normally lend up to 75 percent of the purchase price of the property for buy to let. However, the less you borrow the more favorable terms you can normally get from a bank or building society. This particularly applies now, with the tightening of lending criteria

Buy to Let Mortgages

Buy-to-let (BTL) mortgages are for landlords who buy property to rent it out. The rules around buy-to-let mortgages are similar to those around regular mortgages, but there are some key differences. Read on for more information about how they work, how to get one and what mistakes to avoid.

Who can get a buy-to-let mortgage?

You can get a buy-to-let mortgage if:

- You want to invest in houses or flats.
- You can afford to take a risk. Investing in property is risky, so you shouldn't take out a BTL mortgage if you can't afford to take that risk.
- You already own your own home. You'll struggle to get a buy-to-let mortgage if you don't already own your own home, whether outright or with an outstanding mortgage.
- You have a good credit record and aren't stretched too much on your other borrowings such as your existing mortgage and credit cards.
- You earn £25,000+ a year. Otherwise you might struggle to get a lender to approve your buy-to-let mortgage.
- You're under a certain age. Lenders have upper age limits, typically between 70 or 75. This is the oldest you can be when the mortgage ends not when it starts. For example, if you are 45 when you take out a 25-year mortgage it will finish when you're 70.

How do buy-to-let mortgages work?

Buy-to-let mortgages are a lot like ordinary mortgages, but with some key differences:

- Interest rates on buy-to-let mortgages are usually higher.
- The fees also tend to be much higher.
- The minimum deposit for a buy-to-let mortgage is usually 25% of the property's value (although it can vary between 20-40%).
- Most BTL mortgages are interest-only. This means you don't pay anything each month, but at the end of the mortgage term you repay the capital in full.
- Most BTL mortgage lending is not regulated by the Financial Conduct Authority (FCA). There are exceptions, for example, if you wish to let the property to a close family member (e.g. spouse, civil partner, child, grandparent, parent or sibling). These are often referred to as a consumer buy to let mortgages and are assessed according to the same strict affordability rules as a residential mortgage.

How much you can you borrow for buy-to-let mortgages

The maximum you can borrow is linked to the amount of rental income you expect to receive. Lenders typically need the rental income to be a 25–30% higher than your mortgage payment. To find out what your rent might be talk to local letting agents, or check the local press and online to find out how much similar properties are rented for.

Where to get a buy-to-let mortgage

Most of the big banks and some specialist lenders offer BTL mortgages. It's a good idea to talk to a mortgage broker before you take out a buy-to-let mortgage, as they will help you choose the most suitable deal for you.

Using price comparison websites

Comparison websites are a good starting point for anyone trying to find a mortgage tailored to their needs. the following are the most popular.

* Moneyfacts
* Money Saving Expert
* MoneySuperMarket
* Which?
* Comparison websites won't all give you the same results, so make sure you use more than one site before making a decision. It is also important to do some research into the type of product and features you need before making a purchase or changing supplier.
* Plan for times when there's no rent coming in

Don't assume that your property will always have tenants. There will almost certainly be 'voids' when the property is unoccupied or rent isn't paid and you'll need to have a financial 'cushion' to meet your mortgage payments. When you do have rent coming in, use some of it to top up your savings account. You might also need savings for

19

major repair bills. For example, the boiler might break down, or there may be a blocked drain.

Stamp Duty Land Tax (SDLT)for buy to let properties is an extra 3% on top of the current SDLT rate bands.

Stamp duty- What is stamp duty and who pays it?

Stamp Duty — Stamp Duty Land Tax (SDLT) official jargon — is a tax you pay when you buy a home. The buyer pays stamp duty – not the person selling. Stamp duty applies to both freehold and leasehold purchases over £125,000. However, additional property purchases attract a higher rate, as below:

The current rates of stamp duty from 1st April 2016 for buy to let (additional) properties are;

- 3% tax on the first £125,000
- 5% on the portion up to £250,000
- 8% on the portion up to £925,000
- 13% on the portion up to £1.5 million
- 15% on everything over that

Anyone buying a second property that isn't their main residence will be charged these new rates. This will include holiday lets and buying a property for children if the parents leave their name on the title deeds. Stamp duty has to be paid within 30 days of completion of the purchase of the property although this is usually paid by the solicitor on completion. The amount of Stamp Duty paid is deductible from any capital gains you might make when the property is sold.

Special rates

There are different SDLT rules and rate calculations for:

- corporate bodies
- people buying 6 or more residential properties in one transaction
- shared ownership properties
- multiple purchases or transfers between the same buyer and seller ('linked purchases')
- purchases that mean you own more than one property
- companies and trusts buying residential property

Tax for properties held offshore

HMRC announced in March 2013, that an annual levy will now be made on properties held in British and Offshore companies, costing £2million or more. This is a measure to tackle tax avoidance. Those homes valued at between £2m-£5m will have to pay £15,000 per year; those between £5m-£10m will be taxed at £35,000; those with values of between £10m-£20m will pay £70,000 per year. owners of homes above £20m per year will have to pay £140,000 per year.

Whilst this is not likely to affect readers of this book, it is always better to be aware of such changes.

Other costs

A solicitor normally carries out conveyancing of property. However, individuals can do their own conveyancing, although it isn't as simple as it appears. All the necessary paperwork can be obtained from legal stationers and it is executed on a step-by-step basis. It has to be said that solicitors are now very competitive with their charges and, for the sake of between £600-£900, it is better to let someone else do the work which allows you to concentrate on other things. Another issue will be that your lender will not look favourably on you doing your own conveyancing and will usually insist on the use of a solicitor or licensed conveyancer..

Land Registry

The Land Registry records all purchases of land in England and Wales and is open to the public (inspection of records, called a property search). The registered title to any particular piece of land or property will carry with it a description and include the name of owner, mortgage, rights over other persons land and any other rights. There is a small charge for inspection. A lot of solicitors have direct links and can carry out searches very quickly. Not all properties are registered although it is now a duty to register all transactions.

Capital gains tax

Do you pay Capital Gains Tax on buy to let property?

Yes, if you sell the property for more than you paid for it after deducting costs such as stamp duty and estate agent/solicitors fees. By making a profit, you are essentially 'gaining capital', and so the tax applies. However, as an individual you get an annual allowance to set against any gain.

In the 2017/2018 tax year, this allowance is £11,300. This is a special allowance purely for capital items and is separate from the annual personal income tax allowance. If the gain is greater than the

£11,300 allowance, you will pay tax at a rate of either 18% or 28% on that profit depending on the amount of income and capital gains you have.

Note that the lower CGT rates of 10% and 20% announced in the March 2016 budget do not apply to landlords and buy to let properties.

Energy Performance Certificates (EPC's)

EPC's are compulsory for all rental homes (from 1st October 2008). Therefore all landlords are required to commission an EPC. From 1st of April 2018, privately rented properties must have a rating of E.

As seen above, an EPC surveyor will assess the property and looks at all the ways a house or flat can waste heat, such as inadequate loft insulation, lack of cavity wall insulation, draughts and obsolete boilers. After the assessment they will award a rating from A (as good as it gets) to G (terrible). The document also includes information and advice on how to improve matters, such as lagging the water tank or installing double-glazing. An EPC costs between £120-130 (although shop around and you can get them cheaply or for nothing at all (as part of estate agents inducements) and is valid for ten years. Improvements made while the certificate is in force will not need a new survey.

Examples

There are three examples presented below which will enable the potential investor to get an idea of what problems might be inherent in a range of properties. Obviously, these are three isolated examples but you will get an idea of what to expect.

Example 1 .
The city-centre Flat

Type of house: A two-bedroom flat, built in 1993.

Location: the Jewellery Quarter Birmingham.

Current energy efficient rating: 80% (C)

Potential energy efficiency rating:

82% (B)

Current bills: £198 per year

Potential savings per year: £13

Main failings: Manually controlled heating.

Proposed improvements typically costing less than £500. None

Proposed improvements typically costing more than £500. Install automatically controlled fan-assisted storage heaters, at a cost of about £1,000 for a property of this size (saving £13 per year)

The Georgian Farmhouse

Type of house: Five-bedroom farmhouse, built around 1800.

Location: Ratlinghope near Shrewsbury Shropshire.

Current energy efficiency rating: 30% (F)

Potential energy efficiency rating: 48% (E)

Potential savings: £550 per year.

Main failings: Solid stone walls are not good insulators, the main floor is built directly onto the earth, leaking heat. Only 20% of the windows are double glazed. There is only one energy efficient light bulb.

Proposed improvements costing less than £500. Add 2inches of insulation to the stone walls, at a cost of about £40m square (saving £470 per year) top up loft insulation to 250mm, costing about £240 (saving £58 per year) install low energy lighting (saving £15 per year).

Proposed improvements typically costing £500 or more. Change all windows to double glazing, costing about £350 per window (saving £39 per year) install photovoltaic cells-a typical domestic system costs between £10,000 and £18,000 to install, saving £68 per year.

The London terrace

Type of house: A four-bedroom terraced house built in 1912.

Location: Wandsworth, south London.

Current energy efficient rating: 56% (D).

Current bills: £952 per year.

Potential energy efficient rating: 56% (D).

Potential savings: £247 per year.

Main failings: Solid brick walls without insulation; suspended timber floor; no low-energy lighting; no individually controllable radiators; only 55% double glazing; non-condensing gas boiler.

Proposed improvements typically costing less than £500. Add 2inches of insulation to solid walls, at a cost of about £40 per m2 (saving £170 per year); top up loft insulation by 250mm-cost £240, saving £30 per year; add insulation to hot water tank and pipe-work costing about £300, saving about £19 per year.

Proposed improvements typically costing more than £500 per year. Install thermostatic radiator valves, which cost £250-£300 per radiator saving about £39 per year. Further improvements could be made installing solar water heating-a domestic system will cost £3000-£4,500 to install saving £17 per year.

The above examples were extracted from actual reports and will give an indication of cost and required improvements for specific property types.

Structural surveys

The basic structural survey is the homebuyers' survey and valuation, which is normally carried out by the building society or other lender and it will cost you between £200-350 and is not really an in-depth survey, merely allowing the lender to see whether they should lend or not and how much they should lend. Sometimes lenders keep what they refer to as a retention, which means that they will not forward the full value (less deposit) until certain defined works have been carried out.

If you want to go further than a homebuyers report, and the seller has not included a survey as part of the Home Information Pack (see below) then you will have to instruct a firm of surveyors who have several survey types, depending on how far you want to go and how much you want to spend.

A word of caution. Many people go rushing headlong into buying a flat or house. If you stop and think about this, it is complete folly and can prove very expensive later. A house or flat is a commodity like other commodities, except that it is usually a lot more expensive. A lot can be wrong with the commodity that you have purchased which is not immediately obvious. Only after you have completed the deal and paid over the odds for your purchase do you begin to regret what you have done. The true market price of a property is not what the estate agent is asking, certainly not what the seller is asking. The true market price is the difference between what a property similar to the one in good condition is being sold at and your property minus cost of works to bring it up to that value.

Therefore, if you have any doubts whatsoever, and if you can afford it, get a detailed survey of the property you are proposing to buy and get the works that are required costed out. When negotiating, this survey is an essential tool in order to arrive at an accurate and fair price. Do not rest faith in others, particularly when you alone stand to lose.

One further word of caution. As stated, a lot of problems with property cannot be seen. A structural survey will highlight those. In some cases it may not be wise to proceed at all.

Mortgage arrangement fees

Depending upon the type of mortgage you are considering you may have to pay an arrangement fee. You should budget for anything up to 2% of the purchase price.

Other costs

You should factor in conveyancing costs which can be anything from £500-£1500 depending on the property that you purchase. The solicitor that you employ will give you an idea of the disbursements over and above the basic cost. These disbursements will cover searches of local authorities and utility companies plus other searches as necessary.

****

Chapter 3

Looking For a Property-Location and Type

....

Obviously, where you choose to buy your property to let will be your own decision. However, it may be your first time and you may be at a loss as to where to buy, i.e. rural areas or urban areas, the type and cost of property or whether a house or flat. There are several considerations here. The main consideration for a buy-to-let property is the letting potential and security of your asset, i.e. will it appreciate or will it depreciate.

Area

Buying in a built up area has its advantages and disadvantages. There is usually more demand for property in a built up area. As far as letting is concerned, there are obvious advantages in that there are normally more close communities, because of the sheer density. Local services are closer to hand and there is a greater variety of housing for sale. Transport links are also usually quite good and there are normally plenty of shops.

Disadvantages are less space, less privacy, more local activity, noise and pollution, less street parking, more expensive insurance and different schooling environments to rural environments. The incidence of crime and vandalism and levels of overall stress are higher in built up, more urban areas. This is not the case with all built up areas. It is up to the buyer to carry out research before making a commitment.

If you are thinking of buying to let in a rural area, you might want to consider the following: There is more detached housing with land, more space and privacy. There is also cleaner air and insurance premiums can be lower. Disadvantages can be isolation, loneliness, lower level of services generally, limited choice of local education, therefore the property will be harder to let.

Choosing your property

You should think carefully when considering purchasing a larger property. You may encounter higher costs prior to letting, and also costs that may deter the would be tenant, which may include:

- Larger (more expensive carpeting for example).
- More furniture. If you are letting your property furnished then you will need to outlay more at the outset.
- Larger gardens to tend. Although this may have been one of the attractions, large gardens are time consuming, expensive and hard work.
- Bigger bills.
- More decorating.
- Higher overall maintenance costs.

Purchasing a flat

There are some important points to remember when purchasing a flat. These are common points that are overlooked. For example, if you are buying a flat in a block that is leasehold you will need permission to sublet. This may pose difficulties depending on the freeholder.

Service charge. If you purchase a flat in a block, the costs of maintenance of the flat will be your own. However, the costs of maintaining the common parts will be down to the landlord (usually) paid for by you through a service charge.

There has been an awful lot of trouble with service charges, It has to be said that many landlords see service charges as a way of making profit over and above other income, which is usually negligible after sale of a lease.

Many landlords will own the companies that carry out the work and retain the profit made by these companies. They will charge leaseholders excessively for works, which are often not needed. The 1996 Housing Act, amended by the 2002 Commonhold and Leasehold Reform Act, attempts to strengthen the hand of leaseholders against unscrupulous landlords by making it very difficult indeed for landlords to take legal action for forfeiture (repossession) of lease without first giving the leaseholder a chance to challenge the service charges. In addition, the Acts place an obligation on landlords to be more transparent by producing more detailed accounts and information.

Be very careful if you are considering buying a flat in a block. You should establish levels of service charges and look at accounts. Try to elicit information from other leaseholders.

It could be that there is a leaseholders organisation, formed to manage their own service charges. This will give you direct control over contracts such as gardening, cleaning, maintenance contracts and cyclical decoration contracts. Better value for money is obtained in this way. In this case, at least you know that the levels will be fair, as no one leaseholder stands to profit. All of the above should be considered as the profit that you make from letting your property can be greatly diminished by extra costs such as maintenance charges to a freeholder.

Leasehold Reform Act 1993

Under this Act, as amended by The Commonhold and Leasehold Reform Act 2002, all leaseholders have the right to extend the length of their lease by a term of 90 years. For example, if your lease has 80 years left to run you can extend it to 170 Years. There is a procedure in the above Act for valuation. Leaseholders can collectively also purchase the freehold of the block. There is a procedure for doing this in the Act although it is often time consuming and can be expensive. There are advantages however, particularly when leaseholders are not satisfied with management.

Viewing properties

Before you start house hunting, draw up a list of characteristics you will need from a property, such as the number of bedrooms, size of kitchen, garage and study and garden. Take the estate agents details with you when viewing. Also, take a tape measure with you.

Assess the location of the property. Look at all the aspects and the surroundings. Give some thought as to the impact this will have on the ability to rent.

Assess the building. Check the facing aspect of the property, i.e., north, south etc. Check the exterior carefully. Look for a damp proof course - normally about 15cm from the ground. Look for damp inside and out. Items like leaking rainwater pipes should be noted, as they can be a cause of damp. Look carefully at the windows. Are they rotten? Do they need replacing and so on. Look for any cracks. These should most certainly be investigated. A crack can be symptomatic of something worse or it can merely be surface. If you are not in a position to make this judgment then others should make it for you.

Heating is important. If the house or flat has central heating you will need to know when it was last tested. Gas central heating should be tested at least once a year.

All in all you need to remember that you cannot see everything in a house, particularly on the first visit. A great deal may be being concealed from you. In addition, your own knowledge of property may be slim. A second opinion is a must.

Buying a listed building

Buildings of architectural or historical interest are listed by the Secretary of State for National Heritage following consultation with English Heritage, to protect them against inappropriate alteration. In Wales, buildings are listed by the Secretary of State for Wales in consultation with CADW (Heritage Wales). In Scotland, they are listed by the Secretary of State for Scotland, in consultation with Historic Scotland. If you intend to carry out work to a listed building, you are likely to need listed building consent for any internal or external work, in addition to planning permission. The conservation officer in the local planning department can provide further information.

Buildings in conservation areas

Local authorities can designate areas of special architectural or historical significance. Conservation areas are protected to ensure that their character or interest is retained. Whole towns or villages may be conservation areas or simply one particular street.

Strict regulations are laid down for conservation areas. Protection includes all buildings and all types of trees that are larger than 7cm across at 1.5m above the ground. There may be limitations for putting up signs, outbuilding or items such as satellite dishes. Any developments in the area usually have to meet strict criteria, such as the use of traditional or local materials.

This also applies to property in national parks, designated areas of outstanding natural beauty and the Norfolk or Suffolk Broads.

Whether or not a property is listed or is deemed to be in a conservation area will show up when your conveyancer carries out the local authority search.

Buying a new house

There are a number of benefits to buying a new house. You have the advantages of being the first owner. There should not be a demand for too much maintenance or DIY jobs, as the building is new.

There will however be a defects period, which usually runs for 6 months for building and 12 months for electrical mechanical. During this period you should expect minor problems, such as cracking of walls, plumbing etc, which will be the responsibility of the builder.

Energy loss will be minimal. A new house today uses 50 per cent less energy than a house built 15 years ago; consider the savings over an older property.

An energy rating indicates how energy efficient a house is. The National House Building Council uses a rating scheme based on The

National Energy Services Scheme, in which houses are given a rating between 0 and 10. A house rated 10 will be very energy efficient and have very low running costs for its size. In addition, an Energy Performance Certificate is mandatory, as described earlier. Security and safety are built in to new houses, smoke alarms are standard and security locks on doors and windows are usually included.

When the house market is slow, developers usually offer incentives to buyers, such as cash back, payment of deposit etc.

Building Guarantees

All new houses should be built to certain standards and qualify for one of the building industry guarantees. These building guarantees are normally essential for you to obtain a mortgage and they also make the property attractive to purchasers when you sell. A typical guarantee is the National House Building Council Guarantee (NHBCG).

****

Chapter 4

The Process of Buying a Property

....

Having considered the costs of the acquisition of a property, the next step is to find the property you want. For the investor, as well as all the considerations listed below, the return on investment will be a key priority.

Looking for a property is a long and sometimes dispiriting process. Trudging around estate agents, sorting through mountains of literature, dealing with estate agents details, scouring the papers and walking the streets. However, most of us find the property we want at the end of the day. It is then that we can put in our offer.

Making an offer

You should put your offer in to the estate agent or direct to the seller, depending on who you are buying from.

As discussed earlier, your offer should be based on sound judgment, on what the property is worth and how much rental income after costs that you can derive from it, not on your desire to secure the property at any cost. A survey will help you to arrive at a schedule of works and cost. If you cannot afford to employ a surveyor from a high street firm then you should try to enlist other help. In addition, you should take a long and careful look at the house yourself, not just a cursory glance. Look at everything and try to get an idea of the likely cost to you of rectifying defects. However, I cannot stress enough the importance of getting a detailed survey. Eventually, you will be in a position to make an offer for the property. You should base this offer on sound judgment. You should make it clear that your offer is subject to contract and survey (if you require further examination or wish to carry out a survey after the offer).

Exchange of contracts

Once the buyer and seller are happy with all the details stated in the contract and your conveyancer can confirm that there are no outstanding legal queries, there will be an exchange of contracts. The sale is now legally binding for both parties. You should arrange the necessary insurances, buildings and contents from this moment on, as you are now responsible for the property.

Completing a sale

This is the final day of the sale and normally takes place around ten days after exchange. Exchange and completion can take place on the same day if necessary but this is unusual. On the day of completion, you are entitled to vacant possession and you will receive the keys.

Buying a property at an auction

Property can be purchased in an auction. A small amount of properties are sold in this way. Usually properties sold at auction are either unusual or difficult to put a price on or are repossessions. Auction lists can be obtained from larger estate agents or are advertised in papers. The Estates Gazette, published by the Royal Institute of Chartered Surveyors gives details of auctions in each publication. Normally, this magazine is available to subscribers only, although it can be ordered through a newsagent.

Preparing for auction

Because the auction is the final step of the sale, you should have any conveyancing carried out and your mortgage arranged. Auctions are a quick way of finding a property if you want to buy at undervalue and then renovate the property. It is likely that your choice of property may be limited and you will need to work on it. Many properties at auction are sub standard, this is why they are there in the first place.

- Ask for the package compiled by the auctioneer. It will include full details of the property, and the memorandum of agreement, which is equivalent to the contract.
- View the house.
- Organise a conveyancer and instruct him to carry out searches and arrange surveys.
- If you like the property, set yourself a price limit to bid to, and arrange a mortgage.

Buying before auction

If the sale details quote "unless previously sold" the seller may be prepared to accept offers before the auction, but he will still accept a fast sale and you will be signing an auction contract. You will need to arrange conveyancing and finance very quickly. If you are buying at the auction itself, you should remember that the fall of the hammer on your bid is equivalent to the exchange of contracts as for a private sale. You have made a legal arrangement and you will be expected to pay 10-15 percent deposit on the spot with the remainder of the payment within 28 days.

At the auction

If you are doubtful about your own ability then you can appoint a professional to act on your behalf although they will obviously charge for their services. The seller may be selling subject to a reserve price. If this is the case, it is normally stated in the particulars. The actual figure is not usually disclosed but if the auctioneer states something like "I am going to sell this property today" it is an indication that the reserve price has been reached.

Sale by tender

As an alternative to auction, sale by tender is like a blind auction; you don't know what the other potential buyers are offering. A form of tender is included in the sales details and sometimes sets out the contract details. Always check these details with your conveyancer, because often you cannot pull out after the offer is accepted.

Buyers put their offers in an envelope, sometimes with a 10 percent deposit. These must be received by the seller's agent at a specified date, at which time the seller will accept one of the offers. Sale by tender is sometimes used when there have been two or three offers at similar prices.

****

Chapter 5

Finding a Tenant

....

Whether you are either a landlord or a would - be landlord, you will need to source a tenant for your property. the choice of tenant will be crucial to the success of your business and also for your peace of mind.

Letting Agents

An amendment to the Enterprise and Regulatory Reform Act 2013 enabled the Government to require agents to sign up to a redress scheme. The Redress Scheme for Lettings Agency Work and Property Management Work (Requirement to Belong to a Scheme etc) (England) Order 2014 made membership of a scheme a legal requirement with effect from 1 October 2014. The Government also amended the Consumer Rights Act 2015 to require letting agents to publish a full tariff of their fees. (it should be noted that, If you intend to use an agent to manage your properties then ensure that it is signed up to a redress scheme. One such scheme Is The Property Ombudsman Scheme. www.tpos.co.uk.

Online lettings agents

The rise of online lettings agents has been rapid and they now account for 3.5% of the market. The attractions are obvious, the costs. One of the biggest online property agents, EasyProperty.com offers 'pick and mix' services ranging from £10 a week for adverts on Right Move, Prime Location and Zoopla to 3% commission for full property management. For tenant finding with all the frills, such as hosted viewings and professional photos to check-in the total bill would be £445. This equates to less than half the commission charged by high-street agents. Another agent, Purplebricks.com is also very competitive. However, there can be drawbacks.

The main drawback is accessibility. If you have your contract with a local agent, they will be there when you want them. Online tends to be one step removed. You are strongly advised to consider what it is you want before entering into any deal with an online agent. If you do appoint an agent to manage a property you should agree at the outset, in writing, exactly what constitutes management. Failure to understand the deal can cost you dearly. For example, in a lot of cases, an agent will charge you a fixed fee, sometimes 1 months rental, for finding a tenant, but will then exercise the right that they have given themselves in the initial contract to sign a new agreement and charge another months rent after the tenancy has expired. In this way they will charge you a months rent every six months for doing nothing at all.

What agents do

Agents will typically look after the following:

- Check tenants have the 'Right to Rent' Landlords must ensure tenants can legally reside in the UK before letting to them. The penalty for renting to someone without the right to rent is a £3,000 fine or even imprisonment.

- Give tenants a copy of the 'How to Rent' guide This guide lists landlord obligations and tenants' rights. You must either give tenants a hard copy or email it to them as an attachment. A link to the guide is not enough. Landlords who fail to do this are unable to evict tenants under a Section 21 Notice.
- Transfer the utility bills and the council tax into the name of the tenant. Sign agreements and take up references.
- Paying for repairs, although an agent will only normally do this if rent is being paid directly to them and they can make appropriate deductions.
- Chase rent arrears.
- Serve notices of intent to seek possession if the landlord instructs them to do so. An agent cannot commence court proceedings except through a solicitor.
- Visit the property at regular intervals and check that the tenants are not causing any damage.
- Deal with neighbour complaints.
- Banking rental receipts if the landlord is abroad
- Dealing with housing benefit departments if necessary. The extent to which agents actually do any or all of the above really depends on the caliber of the agent. It also depends on the type of agreement you have with the agent. Like your initial business plan, you should be very clear about what it is you want from the agent and how much they charge.

Beware! There are many so-called rental agencies, which have sprang up since the advent of "Buy to Let". These agents are not professional, do not know a thing about property management, are shady and should be avoided like the plague. Shop around and seek a reputable agent. A typical management fee might be 10-15 percent of the rent, although there is lots of competition and lower prices can be obtained. As stated, there are many ways of charging and you should be clear about this. It is illegal for agencies to charge tenants for giving out a landlord's name and address. Most agencies will charge the landlord.

Advertisements

If you decide to dispense with the use of an agent, the classified advertisement section of local papers is a good place to seek potential tenants. Local papers are obviously cheaper than the nationals such as the Evening Standard in London or the broadsheets such as the Guardian. The type of newspaper you advertise in will largely reflect what type of customer you are looking for. An advert in the pages of the Times would indicate that you are looking for a well-heeled professional and this would be reflected in the type of property that you have to let. There are many free ad papers and also you may want to go to student halls of residence or hospitals in order to attract a potential tenant. When you do advertise, you should indicate clearly the type of property, in what area, what is required, i.e., male or female only, and the rent. You should try and avoid abbreviations as this causes confusion.

- One consideration if looking for a tenant yourself, in October 2014, the new Immigration Act came into force which puts the responsibility on landlords to vet their tenants, or prospective tenants to check to see if they have a right to be in the country.

More information can be obtained from www.gov.uk. In addition, when you have found your prospective tenant you should Give them a copy of the 'How to Rent' guide This guide lists landlord obligations and tenants' rights. You must either give tenants a hard copy or email it to them as an attachment. A link to the guide is not enough. Landlords who fail to do this are unable to evict tenants under a Section 21 Notice.

The public sector

One other source of income is the local authority or housing association. Quite often, your property will be taken off your hands under a five-year contract and you will receive a rental income paid direct for this period, with agreed increases. However, the local authority or housing association will demand a high standard before taking the property off your hands. Quite often the rent achieved will be lower than a comparable market rent, in return for full management and secure income.

If you wish to try this avenue then you should contact your local authority or nearest large association.

Company lets

Where the tenant is a company rather than an individual, the tenancy agreement will be similar to an assured shorthold but will not be bound by the six-month rule (see further on for details of assured shorthold tenancies). Company lets can be from any length of time, from a week to several years, or as long as you like. The major difference between contracts and standard assured shorthold agreements is that the contract

43

will be tailored to individual needs, and the agreement is bound by the provisions of contract law. Company tenancies are bound by the provisions of contract law and not by the Housing Acts. Note: if you are considering letting to a company you must use a letting agent or solicitor. Most companies will insist on it.

The advantages of a landlord letting to a company are:

- A company or embassy has no security of tenure and therefore cannot be a sitting tenant.
- A company cannot seek to reduce the rent by statutory interventions.
- Rental payments are often made quarterly or six monthly in advance.
- The financial status of a company is usually more secure than that of an individual.
- Company tenants often require long-term lets to accommodate staff relocating on contracts of between one and five years.
- The main disadvantages of company lets are:
- A company tenancy can only be to a bona fide company or embassy, not to a private individual.
- A tenancy to a partnership would not count as a company let and may have some security of tenure.
- If the tenant is a foreign government, the diplomatic status of the occupant must be ascertained, as the courts cannot enforce breaches of contract with somebody who possesses diplomatic immunity.
- A tenancy to a foreign company not registered in the UK may

prove time consuming and costly if it becomes necessary to pursue claims for unpaid rent or damage through foreign courts.

Short-lets

Although company lets can be of any length, it is becoming increasingly popular for companies to rent flats from private landlords on short-lets. A short-let is any let of less than six months. But here, it is essential to check the rules with any borough concerned. Some boroughs will not allow lets for less than three months, as they do not want to encourage transient people in the neighborhood.

Generally speaking, short-lets are only applicable in large cities where there is a substantial shifting population. Business executives on temporary relocation, actors and others involved in television production or film work, contract workers and visiting academics are examples of people who might require a short-let.

From a landlord's point of view, short-lets are an excellent idea if you have to vacate your own home for seven or eight months, say, and do not want to leave it empty.

Short-let tenants provide useful extra income as well as keeping an eye on the place. Or if you are buying a new property and have not yet sold the old one, it can make good business sense to let it to a short-let tenant.

Short-let tenants are, usually, from a landlord's point of view, excellent blue-chip occupants. They are busy professionals, high earners, out all day and used to high standards. As the rent is paid by the company there is no worry for the landlord on this score either.

A major plus of short-lets is that they command between 20-50 percent more rent than the optimum market rent for that type of property. The one downside of short-lets is that no agency can guarantee permanent occupancy.

Student lets

Many mainstream letting agencies will not consider students and a lot of landlords similarly are not keen. There is the perception that students will not look after a home and tend to live a lifestyle guaranteed to increase the wear and tear on a property. However, if handled correctly, student lets can be profitable and a number of specialist companies have grown up which concentrate solely on students. Although students quite often want property for only eight or nine months, agencies that deal with students make them sign for a whole year. Rent is guaranteed by confirmation that the student is a genuine student with references from parents, who act as guarantors.

There can be a lot of money made from student lets. However, the tenancy will require more avid policing because of the nature of student lifestyle.

The DSS and housing benefit

Very few letting agencies or landlords will touch DSS or housing benefit tenants. However, as with student lets, there is another side of the coin. Quite often it is essential for a tenant on HB to have a guarantor, usually a homeowner, before signing a tenancy. Then it is up to the machinations of the benefit system to ensure that the landlord receives rent. The rent is assessed by a benefit officer, with the rent usually estimated at market price. There are rent levels set for each are that the benefit officer will not go above.

A deposit is paid normally and rent is paid direct to the landlord. This will require the tenant's consent No other conditions should be accepted by a private landlord. Rent certainly should not be paid direct to the tenant.

Although tenants on HB have a bad name, due to stereotyping, there are many reasons why a person may be on benefit and if housing benefit tenancies are managed well, then this can be a useful source of tenant.

Holiday lets

Before the Housing Act 1988 became law, many landlords advertised their properties as holiday lets to bypass the then rules regarding security of tenure. Strictly speaking, a holiday let is a property let for no more than a month to any one tenant. If the same tenant renews for another month then the landlord is breaking the law. Nowadays, holiday lets must be just that; let for a genuine holiday. If you have a flat or cottage that you wish to let for holiday purposes, whether or not you live in it yourself for part of the year, you are entering into a quite different agreement with the tenant. Holiday lets are not covered by the Housing Act. The contract is finalised by exchange of letters with the tenant where they place a deposit and the owner confirms the booking. If the let is not for a genuine holiday you may have problems in evicting the tenant.

Generally speaking, certain services must be provided for the let to be deemed a holiday let. Cleaning services and changes of bed linen are essential. The amount paid by the holiday-maker will usually include utilities but would exclude use of the telephone, fax machine etc.

If you have a property that you think is suitable for holiday let or wish to invest in one, there are numerous companies who will put you on to their books. However, standards are high and there are a certain number of criteria to be met, such as safety checks, before they will consider taking you on. If possible, you should talk to someone with some experience of this type of let before entering into an agreement with an agency. The usual problems may arise, such as ensuring occupancy all year round and the maintenance of your property, which will be higher due to a high turnover. In addition to the above, the tax situation is changing for those with holiday lets which will mean the loss of certain allowances and the tightening up of others. This is discussed further in chapter 17, which deals with taxation issues.

Letting through Airbnb

Over the last few years, landlords have increasingly turned to companies like Airbnb to let their properties. What started out as a good concept has, as usual been ruined by those looking for a quick return, Airbnb started out as a web based company offering an alternative to hotels, particularly in the overpriced capitals of the world. Landlords now see that there is a profit to be made by allowing a succession of short term tenants to stay in their properties. However, problems have arisen and the courts have found that for landlords with leasehold property to allow their properties to be used by a succession of short term tenants is actually a breach of the lease.

Anyone wishing to let their properties out through companies such as Airbnb should seek advice from their lender, look at their insurance, inform the neighbors and, in London be aware that if you intend to short let your property for more than 90 days you will need planning permission.

Showing the property to the tenant

Once you have found a tenant, the next stage is to make arrangements for viewing the property. It is a good idea to make all appointments on the same day in order to avoid wasting time. If you decide on a likely tenant, it is wise to take up references yourself if you are not using an agency who will do this for you. This will normally be a previous landlord's reference and also a bank reference plus a personal reference. Only when these have been received and you have established that the person(s) is/are safe should you go ahead. Make sure that no keys have been handed over until the cheque has been cleared and you are in receipt of a month's rent and a month's deposit.

Deposits-Tenancy Deposit Protection Scheme

The Tenancy Deposit Protection Scheme was introduced to protect all deposits paid to landlords after 6th April 2007. After this date, landlords and/or agents must use a government authorised scheme to protect deposits. The need for such a scheme has arisen because of the historical problem with deposits. The scheme works as follows:

Moving into a property

At the beginning of a new tenancy agreement, the tenant will pay a deposit to the landlord or agent as usual. Within 30 days the landlord is required to give the tenant details of how the deposit is going to be protected including:

- the address of the rented property
- how much deposit you've paid
- how the deposit is protected
- the name and contact details of the tenancy deposit protection (TDP) scheme and its dispute resolution service
- their (or the letting agency's) name and contact details
- the name and contact details of any third party that's paid the deposit
- why they would keep some or all of the deposit
- how to apply to get the deposit back
- what to do if you can't get hold of the landlord at the end of the tenancy
- what to do if there's a dispute over the deposit

There are three tenancy deposit schemes that a landlord can opt for:

My Deposits

www.mydeposits.co.uk

info@mydeposits.co.uk

0333 321 9401

The Tenancy Deposit Scheme

www.tds.gb.com

0845 226 7837

The Deposit Protection Service

www.depositprotection.com

0330 303 0030

The schemes above fall into two categories, insurance based schemes and custodial schemes.

Custodial Scheme

- The tenant pays the deposit to the landlord
- The landlord pays the deposit into the scheme
- Within 14 days of receiving the deposit, the landlord must give the tenant prescribed information
- A the end of the tenancy, if the landlord and tenant have agreed how much of the deposit is to be returned, they will tell the scheme which returns the deposit, divided in the way agreed by the parties.
- If there is a dispute, the scheme will hold the disputed amount until the dispute resolution service or courts decide what is fair
- The interest accrued by deposits in the scheme will be used to pay for the running of the scheme and any surplus will be used to offer interest to the tenant, or landlord if the tenant isn't entitled to it.

Insurance based schemes

- The tenant pays the deposit to the landlord
- The landlord retains the deposit and pays a premium to the insurer (this is the key difference between the two schemes)

- Within 14 days of receiving a deposit the landlord must give the tenant prescribed information.

- At the end of the tenancy if the landlord and tenant agree how the deposit is to be divided or otherwise then the landlord will return the amount agreed

- If there is a dispute, the landlord must hand over the disputed amount to the scheme for safekeeping until the dispute is resolved

- If for any reason the landlord fails to comply, the insurance arrangements will ensure the return of the deposit to the tenant if they are entitled to it.

If a landlord or agent hasn't protected a deposit with one of the above then the tenant can apply to the local county court for an order for the landlord either to protect the deposit or repay it.

Rental guarantees

The landlord is always advised to obtain a guarantor if there is any potential uncertainty as to payment of rent. One example is where the tenant is on benefits. The guarantor will be expected to assume responsibility for the rent if the tenant ceases to pay at any time during the term of the tenancy. There is a sample guarantee form in the appendix to this book.

****

Chapter 6

What Should Be Provided Under the Tenancy?

....

Furniture

A landlords decision whether or not to furnish property will depend on the sort of tenant that he is aiming to find. The actual legal distinction between a furnished property and an unfurnished property has faded into insignificance. If a landlord does let a property as furnished then the following would be the absolute minimum:

- Seating, such as a sofa and an armchair.
- Cabinet or sideboard.
- Kitchen tables and chairs.
- Cooker and refrigerator.
- Bedroom furniture.

Even unfurnished lets, however, are expected to come complete with a basic standard of furniture, particularly carpets and kitchen goods. If the landlord does supply electrical equipment then he or she will be responsible for carrying out annual checks along with annual checks on the boiler.

Services

Service charges, and the paying of these charges, will be the responsibility of the leaseholder of a flat and will be included in the rent charged by the leaseholder to the tenant of the flat. However, the leaseholder should have some idea of the law in this area as it will be a cost which needs to be considered.

Usually, a landlord (freeholder) will only provide services to a tenant if the property is a flat situated in a block or house split into flats or is a house on a private estate. The services will include cyclical painting and maintenance, usually on a three to four year basis (flats) and gardening and cleaning plus repairs to the communal areas, plus communal electricity bills and water rates. These services should be outlined in the agreement and administered within a strict framework of law. The 1985 Landlord and Tenant Act Section 18-30 as amended by the 1987 LTA and the 1996 Housing Act as amended by the 2002 Commonhold and Leasehold Reform Act are the main areas of law.

The landlord has rigid duties imposed within the Acts, such as the need to gain estimates before commencing works and also to consult with residents where the cost exceeds £250 per flat. The landlord must give the tenant 28 days notice of works to be carried out and a further 28 days to consider estimates, inviting feedback.

Tenants (leaseholders) have the right to see audited accounts and invoices relating to work. Service charges, as an extra payment over and above the rent are always contentious and it is an area that landlords need to be aware of if they are to manage professionally.

Repairs

See chapter on repairs and improvements.

Insurance

Strictly speaking, there is no legal duty on either landlord or tenant to insure the property. However, it is highly advisable for the landlord to provide buildings insurance as he/she stands to lose a lot more in the event of fire or other disaster than the tenant. In addition, mortgagors will always want insurance in place to protect their own investment. A landlord letting property for a first time would be well advised to consult his/her insurance company before letting as there are different criteria to observe when a property is let and not to inform the company could invalidate the policy.

At the end of the tenancy

The tenancy agreement will normally spell out the obligations of the tenant at the end of the term. Essentially, the tenant will have an obligation to:

- Have kept the interior clean and tidy and in a good state of repair and decoration.
- Have not caused any damage.
- Have replaced anything that they have broken.
- Replace or pay for the repair of anything that they have damaged.
- Pay for the laundering of the linen.
- Pay for any other laundering.
- Put anything that they have moved or removed back to how it was.

Sometimes a tenancy agreement will include for the tenants paying for anything that is soiled at their own expense, although sensible wear and tear is allowed for. The landlord will normally be able to recover any loss from the deposit that the tenant has given on entering the premises (see previous chapter for details of the Deposit Protection Schemes). However, sometimes, the tenants will withhold rent for the last month in order to recoup their deposit. The introduction of the Deposit Protection Schemes have made this more difficult in practice. It is up to the landlord to negotiate reimbursement for any damage caused, but this should be within reason. There is a remedy, which can be pursued in the small claims court if the tenants refuse to pay but this is rarely successful.

****

Chapter 7

The Law in a Nutshell

Explaining the law

As a tenant, or potential tenant, it is very important to understand the rights and obligations of both yourself and your landlord, exactly what can and what cannot be done once the tenancy agreement has been signed and you have moved into the property.

Some landlords think they can do exactly as they please, because the property belongs to them. Some tenants do not know any differently and therefore the landlord can, and often does, get away with breaking the law. However there is a very strong legal framework governing the relationship between landlord and tenant and it is important that you have a grasp of the key principles of the law.

In order to fully understand the law we should begin by looking at the main types of relationship between people and their homes.

The freehold and the lease

In law, there are two main types of ownership and occupation of property. These are: freehold and leasehold. These arrangements are very old indeed. In the section dealing with the relationship between leaseholder and freeholder, towards the end of this book, we will be discussing leasehold and freehold in more depth.

Freehold

If a person owns their property outright (usually with a mortgage) then they are a freeholder. The only claims to ownership over and above their own might be those of the building society or the bank, which lent them the money to buy the property. They will re-possess the property if the mortgage payments are not kept up with.

In certain situations though, the local authority (council) for an area can affect a person's right to do what they please with their home even if they are a freeholder. This will occur when planning powers are exercised, for example, in order to prevent the carrying out of alterations without consent.

The local authority for your area has many powers and we will be referring to these regularly.

Leasehold

If a person lives in a property owned by someone else and has a written agreement allowing them to occupy the flat or house for a period of time i.e., giving them permission to live in that property, then they will, in the main, have a lease and either be a leaseholder or a tenant of a landlord.

The main principle of a lease is that a person has been given permission by someone else to live in his or her property for a period of time. The person giving permission could be either the freeholder or another leaseholder. The tenancy agreement is one type of lease. If you have signed a tenancy agreement then you will have been given permission by a person to live in their property for a period of time.

58

The position of the tenant

The tenant will usually have an agreement for a shorter period of time than the typical leaseholder. Whereas the leaseholder will, for example, have an agreement for ninety-nine years, the tenant will have an agreement, which either runs from week to week or month to month (periodic tenancy) or is for a fixed term, for example, six-months or one-year.

These arrangements are the most common types of agreement between the private landlord and tenant.

The agreement itself will state whether it is a fixed term or periodic tenancy. If an agreement has not been issued it will be assumed to be a fixed-term tenancy.

Both periodic and fixed term tenants will usually pay a sum of rent regularly to a landlord in return for permission to live in the property (more about rent and service charges later)

The tenancy agreement

The tenancy agreement is the usual arrangement under which one person will live in a property owned by another. Before a tenant moves into a property he/she will have to sign a tenancy agreement drawn up by a landlord or landlord's agent. *A tenancy agreement is a contract between landlord and tenant.* It is important to realize that when you sign a tenancy agreement, you have signed a contract with another person, which governs the way in which you will live in their property.

The contract

Typically, any tenancy agreement will show the name and address of the landlord and will state the names of the tenant(s). The type of tenancy agreement that is signed should be clearly indicated. This could be, for example, a Rent Act protected tenancy, an assured tenancy or an assured shorthold tenancy. In the main, in the private sector, the agreement will be an assured shorthold.

Date of commencement of tenancy and rent payable

The date the tenancy began and the duration (fixed term or periodic) plus the amount of rent payable should be clearly shown, along with who is responsible for any other charges, such as water rates, council tax etc, and a description of the property you are living in.

In addition to the rent that must be paid there should be a clear indication of when a rent increase can be expected. This information is sometimes shown in other conditions of tenancy, which should be given to the tenant when they move into their home. The conditions of tenancy will set out landlords and tenants rights and obligations.

Services provided under the tenancy and service of notice

If services are provided, i.e., if a service charge is payable, this should be indicated in the agreement. The tenancy agreement should indicate clearly the address to which notices on the landlord can be served by the tenant, for example, because of repair problems or notice of leaving the property. The landlord has a legal requirement to indicate this.

Tenants obligations

The tenancy agreement will either be a basic document with the above information or will be more comprehensive. Either way, there will be a

60

section beginning "the tenant agrees." Here the tenant will agree to move into the property, pay rent, use the property as an only home, not cause a nuisance to others, take responsibility for certain internal repairs, not sublet the property, i.e., create another tenancy, and various other things depending on the property. (The government is, at the moment, actively considering allowing tenants to sublet). It is important that when looking at a tenancy agreement it complies with legislation.

Landlords obligations

There should also be another section "the landlord agrees". Here, the landlord is contracting with the tenant to allow quiet enjoyment of the property. The landlord's repairing responsibilities are also usually outlined.

Ending a tenancy

Finally, there should be a section entitled "ending the tenancy" which will outline the ways in which landlord and tenant can end the agreement. The landlord can only end a fixed term assured shorthold tenancy by issuing a s21 notice (so called because it arises out of section 21 of the Housing Act 1988, as amended) two months prior to the end of the tenancy. Many landlords issued this notice at the outset of the tenancy. However, the Deregulation Act 2015 has effectively stopped this practice and states that the landlord cannot now service the notice until the tenant has been in occupation for at least four months. The tenant, after the expiry of the fixed term, can give one months notice to leave. One more point worth noting is that, if the landlord issues notice, in the required format, by text or email this is likely to be accepted as valid notice.

The landlord must serve a notice by using Form 6A for all tenancies created on or after October 1st 2015. This form must be used for all ASTs created on or after 1 October 2015 except for statutory periodic tenancies which have come into being on or after 1 October 2015 at the end of fixed term ASTs created before 1 October 2015.

See appendix for a sample Form 6A.

It is also in this section of the tenancy that the landlord should make reference to the "grounds for possession". Grounds for possession are circumstances where the landlord will apply to court for possession of his/her property. Some of these grounds relate to what is in the tenancy, i.e., the responsibility to pay rent and to not cause a nuisance. Other grounds do not relate to the contents of the tenancy directly, but more to the law governing that particular tenancy. The grounds for possession are very important, as they are used in any court case brought against the tenant. Unfortunately, they are not always indicated in the tenancy agreement. The sample tenancy agreement in the appendix contains grounds for possession.

It must be said at this point that many residential tenancies are very light on spelling out landlord's responsibilities. For example, repairing responsibilities are landlords obligations under law. This book deals with these obligations, and also other important areas. However, many landlords will seek to use only the most basic document in order to conceal legal obligations. This is one of the main reasons for this book. It is essential that those who intend to let property for profit are able to manage professionally and set high standards as a private landlord. This is because the sector has been beset by rogues in the past. Correspondingly, as a tenant you need to know your rights very clearly and need to know how to enforce them.

The responsibility of the landlord to provide a rent book

If the tenant is a weekly periodic tenant the landlord must provide him/her with a rent book and commits a criminal offence if he/she does not do so. This is outlined in the Landlord and Tenant Act 1985 sections 4 - 7. Under this Act any tenant can ask in writing the name and address of the landlord. The landlord must reply within twenty-one days of asking. As most tenancies nowadays are fixed term assured shortholds then it is not strictly necessary to provide a tenant with a rent book..

However, for the purposes of efficiency, and your own records, it is always useful to have a rent book and sign it each time rent is collected or a standing order is paid.

Overcrowding

It is important to understand, when signing a tenancy agreement, that it is not permitted to allow the premises to become overcrowded, i.e., to allow more people than was originally intended, (which is outlined in the agreement) to live in the property. If a tenant does, then the landlord can take action to evict.

Different types of tenancy agreement

The protected tenancy - the meaning of the term

As a basic guide, if a person is a private tenant and signed their current agreement with a landlord before 15th January 1989 then they will, in most cases, be a protected tenant with all the rights relating to protection of tenure, which are considerable. Protection is provided under the 1977 Rent Act.

In practice, there are not many protected tenancies left and the tenant will usually be signing an assured shorthold tenancy.

The assured shorthold tenancy - what it means

If the tenant entered into an agreement with a landlord after 15th January 1989 then they will, in most cases, be an assured tenant. We will discuss assured tenancies in more depth in chapter three. In brief, there are various types of assured tenancy. The assured shorthold is usually a fixed term version of the assured tenancy and enables the landlord to recover their property after six months and to vary the rent after this time. *It is this tenancy that a private tenant will be signing.*

Other types of agreement

In addition to the above tenancy agreements, there are other types of agreement sometimes used in privately rented property. One of these is the company let, as we discussed in the last chapter, and another is the license agreement. The person signing such an agreement is called a licensee. Licenses will only apply in special circumstances where the licensee cannot be given sole occupation of his home and therefore can only stay for a short period with minimum rights.

64

Chapter 8

Joint Tenancies

_____

Tenancy agreements

A person has a joint tenancy if they and the other tenants all signed a single tenancy agreement with a landlord when they moved in. If each of them signed a separate agreement with the landlord, they have separate tenancies.

Right to rent

As we discussed, a person can only become a private tenant if they have the right to rent. Each joint tenant must have the right to rent. A private landlord or letting agent must carry out a right to rent check before a person/people signs up to a private tenancy.

Paying the rent when you're a joint tenant

Joint tenants are each jointly and individually responsible for paying the rent. If one tenant moves out without giving notice or doesn't pay their share of the rent, the other joint tenants are responsible for paying it for them. If none of them pay the rent, the landlord can ask any one of them to pay the outstanding rent.

Tenancy deposits

The landlord normally takes a single deposit for the whole of the tenancy, even if a tenant and the other joint tenants paid separate or different shares to the landlord or agent. If one joint tenant fails to pay their share of the rent or if they cause damage to the property, the landlord is entitled to deduct the shortfall or the costs of the damage from the whole deposit.

The joint tenants decide how to divide up the remaining deposit when it is returned.

Tenancy deposits when a joint tenant moves out

If a person is replacing another tenant who is moving out, they may ask the incoming person to pay the deposit to them instead. This could cause problems. If the tenant who is moving out has caused any damage to the property or left any unpaid bills, the landlord can deduct these costs from the deposit when they move out.

How tenants can end a fixed-term joint tenancy

If tenants have a fixed-term tenancy (for example for 12 months) they can only the tenancy before the fixed term ends if:

- they, the other tenants and the landlord all agree that the tenancy can end early (this is called a 'surrender')
- there is a 'break clause' in the tenancy agreement, which allows them to give notice and end the tenancy early

A tenant will need the agreement of the other joint tenants to end their tenancy early.

How to end a joint tenancy that isn't a fixed-term

If tenants don't have fixed-term tenancy or it has ended and not been renewed, any joint tenant can end the tenancy by giving a valid notice to quit to the landlord. They can do this with or without the agreement of the other joint tenants. The tenancy ends for all the joint tenants. When the notice to quit expires none of them has the right to continue living there.

Leaving a joint tenancy

If one tenant wants to leave a joint tenancy and the others want to stay they should discuss it with the other joint tenants before they take any action. If they don't want to move out, they can try to negotiate a new agreement with the landlord. The remaining tenants may be able to find another person to become a joint tenant with them. They must get the landlord's agreement for this. Or the remaining tenants could all agree to stay on and pay the rent between them.

However if the joint tenancy has not been ended the landlord could still ask them to pay any arrears if the rent is not fully paid, even if they are no longer living there.

Eviction of joint tenants

The landlord cannot evict one joint tenant without evicting all the others. The landlord may be able to end the tenancy and offer a new one to the remaining tenants.

*

Relationship breakdown

The landlord could grant a new tenancy in the remaining tenant name only if the joint tenancy with an ex-partner has been properly ended. The tenant may also have other rights. For example:

- it may be possible for court to transfer the tenancy into a single name – even if the other joint tenant won't agree to it
- it may be possible to stop the other joint tenant from ending the tenancy by applying for an occupation order or an injunction
- if tenants have experienced domestic violence, it may be possible to take legal action such as an injunction

Problems with other joint tenants

If there are problems with another joint tenant in the first instance tenants have to sort this out themselves. Landlords are usually reluctant to get involved, although council or housing associations are more likely to get involved than private landlords.

****

Chapter 9

Rent and Other Charges

The payment of rent and other financial matters

If a tenancy is protected under the Rent Act 1977, as described earlier there is the right to apply to the Rent Officer for the setting of a fair rent for the property. However, as described earlier, the incidence of Rent Act Protected Tenancies has diminished to almost zero.

The assured tenant

The assured tenant has far fewer rights in relation to rent control than the protected tenant. The Housing Act 1988 allows a landlord to charge whatever he likes. There is no right to a fair or reasonable rent with an assured tenancy. If the tenancy is assured then there will usually be a formula in the tenancy which will provide guidance for rent increases. If not then the landlord can set what rent he or she likes within reason. If the amount is unreasonable then the tenant can refer the matter to the local Rent Assessment Committee. The rent can sometimes be negotiated at the outset of the tenancy. This rent has to be paid as long as the contractual term of the tenancy lasts. Once the contractual term has expired, the landlord is entitled to continue to charge the same rent.

On expiry of an assured shorthold the landlord is free to grant a new tenancy and set the rent to a level that is compatible with the market. Details of the local Rent Assessment Committee can be obtained from the Rent Officer Service at your local authority.

Local housing allowance (LHA) (housing benefit) for people who rent a home from a private landlord.

Local housing allowance is housing benefit for private sector tenants. It's usually paid directly to the tenant and they pay the landlord. Local housing allowance is housing benefit that helps pay the rent and some service charges (if applicable). It's a benefit administered by the local council. LHA has many of the same rules as housing benefit, but there are some extra rules that limit the amount of help tenants can get for a private rented home.

Claim LHA

Tenants can claim local housing allowance if they are a private tenant who needs help with paying the rent. They may be entitled to this housing benefit if they are working or if they claim benefits. Local Housing Allowance (LHA) is used to work out Housing Benefit for tenants who rent privately. How much they get is usually based on:

- where they live
- their household size
- their income - including benefits, pensions and savings (over £6,000)
- their circumstances

The LHA claim is routinely reassessed after 12 months. Their claim may be reassessed at any time if your circumstances change.

How LHA is calculated

The amount of LHA a person can get depends on their income and savings and if any non-dependants live with them, for example adult children. The amount of LHA they receive also depends on the maximum rent allowed for properties in their area and the number of rooms the council decides they need.

They can rent a home of any size or price, but their housing benefit claim is limited. they have to make up any rent shortfall.

Maximum LHA amounts

There are limits on the amount of LHA a person can get. The maximum weekly LHA rate limits (2017-2018) are:

£260.64 for a room in shared accommodation
£260.64 for 1 bedroom accommodation
£302.33 for 2 bedroom accommodation
£354.46 for 3 bedroom accommodation
£417.02 for 4 bedroom accommodation

The amount of LHA they are eligible for depends on where they live. Local limits are based on the cheapest 30% of properties in an area.

Rooms allowed when calculating LHA

A person is assessed as needing a bedroom for the following people in their home:

- an adult couple

- another person aged 16 or over
- any two children of the same sex up to the age of 16
- any two children regardless of sex under the age of 10
- any other child

An extra bedroom can be allowed if a person:

- has a foster child or children
- has a severely disabled child who needs their own room
- the person or their partner are disabled and a carer provides regular overnight care
- has a child who is away on duty with the armed forces and intends to return home
- A person cannot be allowed more than four bedrooms for the purposes of calculating LHA.

If e aged under 35

A person is usually only entitled to LHA at the reduced shared accommodation rate if they are a single person under age 35 without children or live in shared accommodation.

How often is housing benefit paid?

Payment of housing benefit depends on how often the tenant pays rent. Housing benefit is not paid in advance. Each payment covers a past period.

When LHA can be paid direct to landlords

The council must make LHA payments direct to the landlord if:

- the tenant has rent arrears of eight weeks or more
- deductions are being made from their benefits for rent arrears
- In some cases, the council can choose to pay the LHA direct to the landlord. They could do this if the tenant has failed to pay the rent in the past or they have problems paying their rent because of a medical condition. The council can pay LHA direct to the landlord if this will help the tenant keep their tenancy.

If a tenant has support needs, the council can pay LHA to their landlord to encourage them to keep the person as a tenant.

Council Tax Support

If the tenant is in receipt of benefits they may get help with their council tax through Council tax Support.

****

Chapter 10

The Right to Quiet Enjoyment of a Home

Earlier, we saw that when a tenancy agreement is signed, the landlord is contracting to give quiet enjoyment of the tenants home. This means that they have the right to live peacefully in the home without harassment.

The landlord is obliged not to do anything that will disturb the right to the quiet enjoyment of the home. The most serious breach of this right would be for the landlord to wrongfully evict a tenant.

Eviction: what can be done against unlawful eviction

It is a criminal offence for a landlord unlawfully to evict a residential occupier (whether or not a tenant!). The occupier has protection under the Protection from Eviction Act 1977 section 1(2). If the tenant or occupier is unlawfully evicted his/her first course should be to seek an injunction compelling the landlord to readmit him/her to the premises. It is an unfortunate fact but many landlords will attempt to evict tenants forcefully. In doing so they break the law.

The Deregulation Act 2015 has introduced a new provision which deals with 'retaliatory evictions'. This is where the landlord has decided to issue a s21 notice on the tenant because they have complained about the landlords service (for example repairs to the property) or unreasonable behaviour. If it can be proven that the notice was a 'retaliatory notice' then this will be invalid.

However, the landlord may, on termination of the tenancy, recover possession without a court order if the agreement was entered into after 15th January 1989 and it falls into one of the following six situations:

- The occupier shares any accommodation with the landlord and the landlord occupies the premises as his or her only or principal home.

- The occupier shares any of the accommodation with a member of the landlords family, that person occupies the premises as their only or principal home, and the landlord occupies as his or her only or principal home premises In the same building.

- The tenancy or license was granted temporarily to an occupier who entered the premises as a trespasser.

- The tenancy or license gives the right to occupy for the purposes of a holiday.

- The tenancy or license is rent-free.

- The license relates to occupation of a hostel.

There is also a section in the 1977 Protection from Eviction Act which provides a defense for otherwise unlawful eviction and that is that the landlord may repossess if it is thought that the tenant no longer lives on the premises. It is important to note that, in order for such action to be seen as a crime under the 1977 Protection from Eviction Act, the intention of the landlord to evict must be proved. However, there is another offence, namely harassment, which also needs to be proved. Even if the landlord is not guilty of permanently depriving a tenant of their home he/she could be guilty of harassment. Such actions as cutting off services, deliberately allowing the premises to fall into a state of disrepair, or even forcing unwanted sexual attentions, all constitute harassment and a breach of the right to *quiet enjoyment*.

The 1977 Protection from Eviction Act also prohibits the use of violence to gain entry to premises. Even in situations where the landlord has the right to gain entry without a court order it is an offence to use violence.

Remedies against unlawful eviction?

There are two main remedies for unlawful eviction: damages and, as stated above, an injunction.

The injunction

An injunction is an order from the court requiring a person to do, or not to do something. In the case of eviction the court can grant an injunction requiring the landlord to allow a tenant back into occupation of the premises. In the case of harassment an order can be made preventing the landlord from harassing the tenant. Failure to comply with an injunction is contempt of court and can result in a fine or imprisonment.

Damages

In some cases the tenant can press for *financial compensation* following unlawful eviction. Financial compensation may have to be paid in cases where financial loss has occurred or in cases where personal hardship alone has occurred. The tenant can also press for *special damages,* which means that the tenant may recover the definable out-of-pocket expenses. These could be expenses arising as a result of having to stay in a hotel because of the eviction. Receipts must be kept in that case. There are also *general damages*, which can be awarded in compensation for stress, suffering and inconvenience.

A tenant may also seek *exemplary damages* where it can be proved that the landlord has disregarded the law deliberately with the intention of making a profit out of the displacement of the tenant.

****

Chapter 11

Repairs-Landlords/Tenants Obligations

Repairs and improvements generally: The landlord and tenants obligations

Repairs are essential works to keep the property in good order. Improvements and alterations to the property, e.g. the installation of a shower.

As we have seen, most tenancies are periodic, i.e. week-to-week or month-to-month. If a tenancy falls into this category, or is a fixed-term tenancy for less than seven years, and began after October 1961, then a landlord is legally responsible for most major repairs to the flat or house.

If a tenancy began after 15th January 1989 then, in addition to the above responsibility, the landlord is also responsible for repairs to common parts and service fittings.

The area of law dealing with the landlord and tenants repairing obligations is the 1985 Landlord and Tenant Act, section 11. This section of the Act is known as a covenant and cannot be excluded by informal agreement between landlord and tenant. In other words the landlord is legally responsible whether he or she likes it or not. Parties to a tenancy, however, may make an application to a court mutually to vary or exclude this section.

Example of repairs a landlord is responsible for:

- Leaking roofs and guttering.
- Rotting windows.
- Rising damp.
- Damp walls.
- Faulty electrical wiring.
- Dangerous ceilings and staircases.
- Faulty gas and water pipes.
- Broken water heaters and boilers.
- Broken lavatories, sinks or baths.

In shared housing the landlord must see that shared halls, stairways, kitchens and bathrooms are maintained and kept clean and lit.

Normally, tenants are responsible only for minor repairs, e.g., broken door handles, cupboard doors, etc. Tenants will also be responsible for decorations unless they have been damaged as a result of the landlord's failure to do repair.

A landlord will be responsible for repairs only if the repair has been reported. If the repair is not carried out then action can be taken. Damages can also be claimed.

Compensation can be claimed, with the appropriate amount being the reduction in the value of the premises to the tenant caused by the landlord's failure to repair. If the tenant carries out the repairs then the amount expended will represent the decrease in value.

The tenant does not have the right to withhold rent because of a breach of repairing covenant by the landlord. However, depending on the

79

repair, the landlord will not have a very strong case in court if rent is withheld.

Reporting repairs to landlords

The tenant has to tell the landlord or the person collecting the rent straight away when a repair needs doing. It is advisable that it is in writing, listing the repairs that need to be done.

Once a tenant has reported a repair the landlord must do it within a reasonable period of time. What is reasonable will depend on the nature of the repair. If certain emergency work needs to be done by the council, such as leaking guttering or drains a notice can be served ordering the landlord to do the work within a short time. In exceptional cases if a home cannot be made habitable at reasonable cost the council may declare that the house must no longer be used, in which case the council has a legal duty to re-house a tenant.

If after the council has served notice the landlord still does not do the work, the council can send in its own builder or, in some cases take the landlord to court. A tenant must allow a landlord access to do repairs. The landlord has to give twenty-four hours notice of wishing to gain access.

The tenants rights whilst repairs are being carried out

The landlord must ensure that the repairs are done in an orderly and efficient way with minimum inconvenience to the tenant. If the works are disruptive or if property or decorations are damaged the tenant can apply to the court for compensation or, if necessary, for an order to make the landlord behave reasonably.

If the landlord genuinely needs the house empty to do the work he/she can ask the tenant to vacate it and can if necessary get a court order against the tenant. A written agreement should be drawn up making it clear that the tenant can move back in when the repairs are completed and stating what the arrangements for fuel charges and rent are. If a person is an assured tenant the landlord could get a court order to make that person give up the home permanently if there is work to be done with him/her in occupation.

Can the landlord put the rent up after doing repairs?

If there is a service charge for maintenance, the landlord may be able to pass on the cost of the work(s).

Tenants rights to make improvements to a property

Unlike carrying out repairs the tenant will not normally have the right to insist that the landlord make actual alterations to the home. However, a tenant needs the following amenities and the law states that they should have:

- Bath or shower.
- Wash hand basin.
- Hot and cold water at each bath, basin or shower.
- An indoor toilet.

If these amenities do not exist then the tenant can contact the council's Environmental Health Officer. An improvement notice can be served on the landlord ordering him to put the amenity in.

81

Disabled tenants

If a tenant is disabled he/she may need special items of equipment in the accommodation. The local authority may help in providing and, occasionally, paying for these. The tenant will need to obtain the permission of the landlord. If you require more information then contact the social services department locally.

The Equality Act 2010

The Equality Act 2010 has introduced a new duty on landlords (from October 2010) to consent to changes in common parts of residential or mixed-use buildings in England, Wales and Scotland. This means that if a disabled tenant or occupier who uses or intends to use premises in a building as his or her main home requests physical changes to common parts to reduce or avoid a disadvantage suffered in comparison with non-disabled people, the landlord must within a reasonable time consult all other likely to be affected by the changes and, having considered the views of those consulted, take whatever steps are reasonable to avoid the disadvantage.

If changes to the common parts are considered reasonable the landlord must first enter into a written agreement that the disabled person organizes and pays for the work and for restoration of the common parts when the disabled person leaves the property.

The agreement will bind the landlord's successors but not the disabled person's successors. So the landlord may wish to insist that the works are reinstated before the disabled person leaves.

Shared housing. The position of tenants in shared houses (Houses in Multiple Occupation)

A major change to improve standards of shared housing was introduced in 2006. The parts of the Housing Act 2004 relating to the licensing of HMO's (Houses in Multiple Occupation) and the new Health and Safety Rating System for assessing property conditions came into effect on 6rh April 2006. The Act requires landlords of many HMO's to apply for licences. The HMO's that need to be licensed are those with:

- Three or more storeys, which are
- Occupied by five or more people forming two or more households (i.e. people not related, living together as a couple etc) and
- Which have an element of shared facilities (eg kitchen, bathroom etc)

As far as licensing is concerned, attics and basements are included as storeys if they are used as living accommodation. Previously, HMO's were only defined as houses converted into flats or bedsits, but the new Act widens this definition and many more types of shared houses are now included.

A local authority will have a list of designated properties will have a list of those properties which are designated HMO's and they will need to be licensed.

Usually, landlords will need to apply to a local authority private sector unit for licences. It has been illegal for landlords to manage designated properties without a licence since July 2006.

Landlords will have to complete an application form and pay a fee, the local authority will then assess whether the property is suitable for the number of people the landlord wants to rent it to. In most case, the local authority, their agents, will visit a property to assess facilities and also fire precautions. A decision will then be taken to grant a license. There is a fee for registration, councils set the fee and the ones shown below are indicative of a southern local authority:

Shared houses-five sharers landlords first house £640

Subsequent house £590

Plus £10 each additional occupier over five

Hostels

10 occupiers £690

20 occupiers £790

50 occupiers £1100

75 occupiers £1340

In summary, The landlord of a HMO has certain duties under the regulations to his tenants:

Duty to provide information

The manager (this means that whoever is charged with the management of the building) must ensure that:

- His name, address and telephone number are available to each household in the HMO
- These details are also clearly displayed in a prominent position in the HMO.

The manager should maintain a log book to record all events at the property such as:

- Testing of fire alarms
- Testing of fire fighting equipment
- Gas safety certificate
- Electrical report
- Inspection and wants of repair

Duty to take safety measures

The manager must ensure that all means of escape from fire in the property are kept free from obstruction and in good order as should all fire alarms and equipment. The manager should ensure that the structure is designed and maintained in a safe condition, and also take steps to protect occupiers from injury. In properties with four or more occupants, the Regulations provide that fire escape notices be clearly displayed.

Duty to maintain water supply drainage

The manager must ensure that the water supply and drainage system serving the property are maintained in a good working condition. More specifically, water fittings should be protected from frost and all water storage tanks should be provided with covers.

Duty to supply and maintain gas and electricity

The manager must supply the local housing authority within 7 days of receiving a written request a safety certificate. The manager must ensure that the fixed electrical installation is checked at least once every three years by a suitably qualified electrician and supply this to the LHA on written request. In addition to the above, there is a duty to maintain common parts, fixtures, fittings and appliances. There is a duty to maintain living accommodation and to provide waste disposal facilities.

Powers of the local authority in relation to HMO's

It is essential to ensure that, if you have invested in a HMO that you manage it rigorously because local authorities have sweeping powers to fine landlords and to revoke licenses. A local authority can prosecute a landlord who does not obtain a license for a HMO.

Safety generally for all landlords-the regulations

The main product safety regulations relevant to the lettings industry are:

Gas safety

The Gas safety (Installation and use) Regulations 1998
The Gas Cooking Appliances (safety) Regulations 1989
Heating Appliances(Fireguard) (safety) Regulations 1991
Gas Appliances(Safety) Regulations 1995

All of the above are based on the fact that the supply of gas and the appliances in a dwelling are safe. A Gas Safety certificate is required to validate this.

Furniture Safety

Furniture and Furnishings (Fire) (Safety) Regulations 1988 and 1993 (as amended). Landlords and lettings agents are included in these regulations. The regulations set high standards for fire resistance for domestic upholstered furniture and other products containing upholstery.

The main provisions are:

- Upholstered articles (i.e. beds, sofas, armchairs etc) must have fire resistant filling material.
- Upholstered articles must have passed a match resistant test or, if of certain kinds (such as cotton or silk) be used with a fire resistant interliner.
- The combination of the cover fabric and the filling material must have passed a cigarette resistance test.

The landlord should inspect property for non-compliant items before letting and replace with compliant items.

Electrical Safety
Electrical Equipment (Safety) Regulations 1994
Plugs and Sockets etc. (Safety) Regulations 1994.

The Electrical Equipment Regulations came into force in January 1995. Both sets of regulations relate to the supply of electrical equipment designed with a working voltage of between 50 and 1000 volts a.c. (or between 75 and 1000 volts d.c.) the regulations cover all the mains voltage household electrical goods including cookers, kettles, toasters, electric blankets, washing machines, immersion heaters etc. The regulations do not apply to items attached to land. This is generally considered to exclude the fixed wiring and built in appliances (e.g. central heating systems) from the regulations.

The availability of grants

Disabled Facilities Grant

The only mandatory grant is the Disabled Facilities Grant, given to those in need, which has been assessed by an Occupational Therapist-the grant has a ceiling. Information of which can be obtained from the local authority. As the name suggests it is for those who are disabled and are n need of works which will make the property accessible and usable for disabled people. For information about other grants available contact the local authority dealing with your area.

New regulations on Smoke and Carbon Monoxide detectors

From October 2015, all landlords, regardless of whether public or private sector, will be required to install working smoke and carbon monoxide alarms in their properties, on each floor. The carbon monoxide alarms will need to be placed in high risk areas, i.e., where there are gas appliances such as boilers or fires. Carbon monoxide detectors will not be required in properties where there are no gas or solid fuel appliances. A civil penalty of up to £5,000 will apply to landlords who fail to comply with this legislation.

Sanitation health and hygiene

Local authorities have a duty to serve an owner with a notice requiring the provision of a WC when a property has insufficient sanitation, sanitation meaning toilet waste disposal. They will also serve notice if it is thought that the existing sanitation is inadequate and is harmful to health or is a nuisance.

Local authorities have similar powers under various Public Health Acts to require owners to put right bad drains and sewers, also food storage facilities and vermin, plus the containing of disease. The Environmental Health Department, if it considers the problem bad enough will serve a notice requiring the landlord to put the defect right. In certain cases the local authority can actually do the work and require the landlord to pay for it. This is called work in default.

****

Chapter 12

Regaining Possession of a Property

....

Fast-track possession

Previously, a landlord will have served a section 21 notice on the tenant at the start of the tenancy. However, following the passage of the Deregulation Act 2015, the landlord can no longer do this and must serve the notice after the tenant has been in occupation for four months. This brings the tenancy to an end on the day of expiry, i.e. on the day of expiry of the six month period, or 12 month period, whichever is appropriate. It should be noted that if a landlord takes a deposit from the tenant then every deposit must be registered with the appropriate deposit service before the landlord can serve the s21 notice.

It should also be noted that if a section 21 notice is served after the end of the fixed term giving two months notice then the notice should be a section 21 (b). This is important as a service of the incorrect notice can delay proceedings. For all AST's issued after October 1st 2015, a Form 6a is served (se appendix).

On expiry of the notice, if it is the landlord's intention to take possession of the property then the tenants should leave. It is worthwhile writing a letter to the tenants one month before expiry reminding them that they should leave.

In the event of the tenant refusing to leave, then the landlord has to then follow a process termed 'fast track possession'. This entails filling in the appropriate forms (N5B) which can be accessed from:

www.gov.uk/accelerated-possession-eviction. the process is online and costs £355 (2017/2018)

Assuming that a valid section 21 notice has been served on the tenant, the accelerated possession proceedings can begin and the forms completed online which are then lodged with the court dealing with the area where the property is situated. In order to grant the accelerated possession order the court will require the following:

The assured shorthold agreement

The section 21 notice (or form 6a)

Evidence of service of the section 21 notice

The best form of service of the s21 notice is by hand. If the notice has already served then evidence that the tenant has received it will be required. A copy must also be served on the tenant. This will be done by the court although it might help if the landlord also serves a copy informing the tenant that they are taking proceedings. If the tenant disputes the possession proceedings in any way they will have 14 days to reply to the court. If the case is well founded and the paperwork is in order then there should be no case for defence. Once the accelerated possession order has been granted then this will need to be served on the tenant, giving them 14 days to vacate. In certain circumstances, if the tenant pleads hardship the court can grant extra time to leave, six weeks as opposed to two weeks. If they still do not vacate then an application will need to be made to court for a bailiffs warrant to evict the tenants.

An accelerated possession order remains in force for six years from the date it was granted.

Going to court to end the tenancy

There may come a time when the landlord needs to go to court to regain possession of a property. This will usually arise when the contract has been breached by the tenant, for non-payment of rent or for some other breach such as nuisance or harassment. As we have seen, a tenancy can be brought to an end in a court on one of the grounds for possession. However, as the tenancy will usually be an assured shorthold then it is necessary to consider whether the landlord is in a position to give two months notice and withhold the deposit, as opposed to going to court. The act of withholding the deposit will entail the landlord refusing to authorize the payment to the tenant online. This then brings arbitration into the frame. Deposit schemes have an arbitration system as an integral part of the scheme.

If the landlord decides, for whatever reason, to go to court, then any move to regain the property for breach of agreement will commence in the county court in the area in which the property is. The first steps in ending the tenancy will necessitate the serving of a notice of seeking possession using one of the Grounds for Possession detailed earlier in the book. If the tenancy is protected then 28 days must be given, the notice must be in prescribed form and served on the tenant personally (preferably).

If the tenancy is an assured shorthold, which is more often the case now, then 14 days notice of seeking possession can be used. In all cases the ground to be relied upon must be clearly outlined in the notice. If the case is more complex, then this will entail a particulars of claim being prepared, usually by a solicitor, as opposed to a standard possession form.

A fee is paid when sending the particulars to court, which should be checked with the local county court. The standard form which the landlord uses for routine rent arrears cases is called the N119 and the accompanying summons is called the N5. Both of these forms can be obtained from the court or from :

justice.gov.uk/HMCTS/FormFinder.do When completed, the forms should be sent in duplicate to the county court and a copy retained for the landlord.

The court will send a copy of the particulars of claim and the summons to the tenant. They will send the landlord a form which gives him a case number and court date to appear, known as the return date.

On the return date, the landlord will arrive at court at least 15 minutes early. He can represent yourself in simple cases but will be advised to use a solicitor for more contentious cases.

If the tenant is present then they will have a chance to defend themselves.

A number of orders are available. However, if a landlord has gone to court on the mandatory ground eight then if the fact is proved then they will get possession immediately. If not, then the judge can grant an order, suspended whilst the tenant finds time to pay.

In a lot of cases, it is more expedient for a landlord to serve notice-requiring possession, if the tenancy has reached the end of the period, and then wait two months before the property is regained. This saves the cost and time of going to court particularly if the ground is one of nuisance or other, which will involve solicitors.

If the landlord regains possession of your property midway through the contractual term then he will have to complete the possession process by use of bailiff, pay a fee and fill in another form, Warrant for Possession of Land.

****

Chapter 13

Private Tenancies in Scotland

The law governing the relationship between private landlords and tenants in Scotland is different to that in England. Since the beginning of 1989, new private sector tenancies in Scotland have been covered by the Housing (Scotland) Act 1988. Following the passage of this Act, private sector tenants no longer have any protection as far as rent levels are concerned and tenants enjoy less security of tenure. However, **The Private Housing (Tenancies) (Scotland) Act 2016**, passed by the Scottish Parliament and coming into force at the end of 2017 may have some bearing in this area. The main provisions of the Act are outlined at the end of this chapter.

Short assured and assured tenancies

Most residential lettings in Scotland made after 2 January 1989 are short assured tenancies. Those that aren't short assured are normally assured tenancies.

Short assured tenancies

This is the most common type of tenancy. A short assured tenancy makes it easier for a landlord to get a property than an assured tenancy. Before any agreement is signed, a landlord must use form AT5 to tell new tenants that the tenancy will be a short assured tenancy. (see appendix). If they don't, the tenancy will automatically be an assured tenancy. Initially, a short assured tenancy must be for 6 months or more. After the first 6 months, the tenancy can be renewed for a shorter period.

Assured tenancies

At the beginning of an assured tenancy, it will be classed as a 'contractual assured tenancy' for a fixed period of time. The tenancy automatically becomes a 'statutory assured tenancy' if:

- the landlord ends the tenancy by issuing a notice to quit (eg because they want to change the agreement) and the tenant stays in the property
- the fixed period covered by the tenancy comes to an end and the tenant stays in the property

There are different rights and responsibilities on both landlord and tenant depending on the type of assured tenancy.

Other types of tenancy

Most tenancies in Scotland are short assured or assured tenancies. The other tenancy types are:

- 'common law' tenancy - if a tenant shares their home as a lodger
- regulated tenancy - the most common form of tenancy before 1989
- agricultural tenancy

- crofting tenancy

'Common law' tenancies

If a landlord is sharing their house or flat with their tenants, they can't use the short assured or assured tenancy. Instead, they will automatically have what is known as a 'common law tenancy'. The tenant doesn't have to have a written contract but the landlord may use a lodger agreement to create a contract between them and the tenant - so both are clear about what has been agreed. (see appendix for sample lodger agreement).

Regulated tenancies

Tenancies created before 2 January 1989 are generally regulated tenancies. As not many exist we will not be describing them further here.

Agricultural tenancies

There are 3 types of agricultural tenancy:

- limited duration tenancy - if the lease is for more than 5 years
- short limited duration tenancy - if the lease is for 5 years or less
- 1991 Act tenancy - if the tenancy began before 2003

All agricultural tenants have the right to:

- a written lease
- compensation at the end of the tenancy for any improvements

they made to the land during their tenancy

- leave the tenancy to a spouse or relative in their will

If the lease is over 5 years, agricultural tenants can also:

- pass their tenancy on to a relative or spouse within their lifetime
- use the land for non-agricultural purposes
- Tenants with a 1991 Act tenancy have the right to buy the land they are leasing.

If there's a house on the land, both landlord and tenant have obligations to keep it in good repair.

Crofting tenancies

Crofting is a system of landholding unique to the Highlands and Islands of Scotland. Usually, the crofter holds the croft on the 'statutory conditions' and doesn't have a written lease. Crofting is regulated by the Crofting Commission. The tenant must get written agreement from the Commission if you want to make any changes to a crofting tenancy (including a change of tenant).

What the landlord must include in a tenancy agreement

If a landlord uses an assured or short assured tenancy, the agreement must be written down. It must include:

- the names of all people involved
- the rental price and how it's paid

- the deposit amount and how it will be protected (see below)
- when the deposit can be fully or partly withheld (eg to repair damage caused by tenants)
- the property address
- the start and end date of the tenancy
- any tenant or landlord obligations
- who's responsible for minor repairs
- which bills your tenants are responsible for
- a statement telling the tenant that antisocial behaviour is a breach of the agreement

For other types of tenancy, it's still good practice to put the agreement in writing. including other information To avoid any confusion later, the landlord can include other information in the agreement, such as:

- whether the tenancy can be ended early and how this can be done
- information on how and when the rent will be reviewed
- whether the property can be let to someone else (sublet) or have lodgers

Changes to tenancy agreements

The landlord must get the agreement of their tenants if they want to make changes to the terms of their tenancy agreement.

*

Preventing discrimination

Unless the landlord have a very strong reason, they must change anything in a tenancy agreement that might discriminate against tenants on the grounds of:

- gender
- sexual orientation
- disability (or because of something connected with their disability)
- religion or belief
- being a transsexual person
- the tenant being pregnant or having a baby

Ending a tenancy

Tenancies don't automatically end when the term of the tenancy agreement comes to an end. To end a tenancy agreement, the landlord must follow the correct procedures starting with a **Notice to quit.** To end any tenancy other than a common law tenancy, a landlord must give tenants a 'notice to quit'. Even for common law tenancies, this is still good practice. Landlords don't have to use a particular form, but for a notice to quit to be valid it must be in writing and must tell tenants:

- how much notice the landlord is giving them
- that the landlord still needs a court order to get their property back if the tenants don't leave when the notice runs out
- that the tenant can get independent advice about the notice - and where they can get that advice from)

Short assured tenancy

To get a property back, the landlord must give tenants a 'notice to quit' and a 'Section 33 notice'. For a short assured tenancy, the minimum notice period is 40 days if the tenancy is for 6 months or longer.

For a tenancy that is continuing on a month by month basis after the original period has ended, the notice period is a minimum of 28 days. The landlord must give 2 months notice when giving a Section 33 notice. They can issue both the notice to quit and Section 33 notice at the same time. (see appendix)

Other tenancy types

For other tenancy types the landlord must give at least:

- 28 days if the tenancy is for up to 1 month
- 31 days if the tenancy is for up to 3 months
- 40 days if the tenancy is for more than 3 months

Ending a tenancy early

A landlord can end a tenancy early if:

- the tenant breaks a condition of the tenancy agreement
- landlord and tenant agree to end the tenancy

If tenants don't leave

If the notice period expires and tenants don't leave the property, the landlord can start the process of eviction through the courts. A landlord must tell tenants of their intention to get a court order by giving them a 'notice of intention to raise proceedings' (AT6) (see appendix).

If tenants want to leave

The tenancy agreement should say how much notice tenants need to give before they can leave the property. If the notice isn't mentioned in the tenancy agreement, the minimum notice a tenant can give is:

- 28 days if their tenancy runs on a month-to-month basis (or if it's for less than a month)
- 40 days if their tenancy is for longer than 3 months

Ending a tenancy early

Unless there's a break clause in the tenancy agreement, a landlord can insist that their tenants pay rent until the end of the tenancy. If tenants leave the property without giving notice, or before the notice has run out, they're still responsible for the property and the rent by law.

Houses in multiple occupation (HMOs)

If a tenant is living in a bedsit, shared flat, lodging, shared house, hostel or bed and breakfast accommodation it's likely that they will be living a house in multiple occupation or 'HMO'. A landlord will have an HMO if:

- tenants live with two or more other people, and
- they don't belong to the same family, and
- they share some facilities, e.g. a bathroom or kitchen, and

- the accommodation is their only or main home (if they are a
  student, their term-time residence counts as their main home).

If they live with a homeowner their family doesnt count as 'qualifying
persons' when deciding whether or not a property is an HMO. So for
example, if they share accommodation with the owner and one other
unrelated lodger, they won't live in an HMO. If they live with the
owner and two other unrelated lodgers, they will live in an HMO.
Before the council gives a landlord an HMO licence, it will carry
out the following checks:

Is the landlord a fit and proper person to hold a licence?

Before it will grant an HMO licence, the council must check that the
owner and anyone who manages the property (for example, a letting
agent) don't have any criminal convictions, for example, for fraud or
theft.

Is the property managed properly?

The council must check that the landlord respects tenants legal rights.
They should be given a written tenancy agreement stating clearly what
the landlord's responsibilities are, and what the tenants responsibilities
are. This should cover things like rent, repairs and other rules. To
manage the property properly, the landlord must:

- keep the property and any furniture and fittings in good repair
- deal with the tenant fairly and legally when it comes to rent and
  other payments, for example they:
- must go through the correct procedure if they want to increase
  the rent

- cannot resell the tenant gas or electricity at a profit
- not evict the tenant illegally
- make sure that their tenants don't annoy or upset other people living in the area.

Does the property meet the required standards?

To meet the standards expected of an HMO property:

- the rooms must be a decent size, for example, every bedroom should be able to accommodate a bed, a wardrobe and a chest of drawers.
- there must be enough kitchen and bathroom facilities for the number of people living in the property, with adequate hot and cold water supplies.
- adequate fire safety measures must be installed, for example the landlord must provide smoke alarms and self-closing fire doors and make sure there is an emergency escape route.
- all gas and electrical appliances must be safe.
- heating, lighting and ventilation must all be adequate.
- the property should be secure, with good locks on the doors and windows.
- there must be a phone line installed so that tenants can set up a contract with a phone company to supply the service.

What are the landlord's responsibilities?

In order to keep their HMO licence, a landlord must maintain the property properly:

- **Common parts** - these must be kept clean and in good repair (for example, the stairwell, hall, shared kitchen and bathroom). However, the landlord can include a clause in the tenancy agreement which passes this responsibility onto the tenants.

- **Shared facilities** - these should be kept in good repair (for example, the cooker, boiler, fridge, sinks, bath and lighting)
- **Heating, hot water and ventilation** - these facilities must all be kept in good order
- **Gas safety** - all gas appliances and installations must be safe (for example, a gas fire, boiler or cooker) - these should be checked once a year by a Gas Safe Register engineer
- **Electrical safety** - all electrical appliances and installations must be safe - these should be tested every three years by a contractor approved by the National Inspection Council for Electrical Installation Contracting (NICEIC) or SELECT, Scotland's trade association for the electrical, electronics and communications systems industry
- **Fire precautions** - all fire precautions (for example, smoke alarms and fire extinguishers) must be in good working order and that the fire escape route is kept safe and free from obstructions
- **Furniture** - all furniture supplied must meet safety standards (for example, isn't flammable)
- **Roof, windows and exterior** - these must all be adequately maintained
- **Rubbish** - enough rubbish bins must be provided
- **Deposits** - tenants deposits must be returned within a reasonable time when they move out, preferably within 14 days.

The landlord should also put up notices in the accommodation:

- giving the name and address of the person responsible for managing it so that the tenant can contact them whenever necessary
- explaining what the tenant should do in an emergency, for example if there is a gas leak or a fire.

Tenants responsibilities:

- **Repairs** – the tenant should let the landlord know if anything in the property needs repairing, particularly if this is something they are responsible for keeping in good order, such as the roof, boiler or toilet
- **Damage** – the tenant must take good care of the property and try not to damage anything
- **Rubbish** - not let rubbish pile up in or around the property but dispose of it properly in the bins provided
- **Inspections** - let the landlord inspect the property so they can check whether any maintenance work needs doing. Normally this should happen once every six months. The landlord must give you 24 hours' written notice before coming round.
- **Behave responsibly** - make sure that the tenant doesnt behave in a way that can annoy or upset neighbours. The landlord is responsible for dealing with any complaints made by neighbours and must take action if they are unhappy with tenants behaviour.

Safeguarding Tenancy Deposits

A tenancy deposit scheme is a scheme provided by an independent third party to protect deposits until they are due to be repaid. Three schemes are now operating:

- Letting Protection Service Scotland
- Safedeposits Scotland
- Mydeposits Scotland

Landlord's legal duties

The legal duties on landlords who receive a tenancy deposit are:

- to pay deposits to an approved tenancy deposit scheme
- to provide the tenant with key information about the tenancy and deposit

Key dates for landlords

The dates by which landlords must pay deposits to an approved scheme and provide information to the tenant vary, depending on when the deposit was received:

1. Deposit received prior to 7 March 2011:

Where the tenancy is renewed by express agreement or tacit relocation on or after 2 October 2012 and before 2 April 2013 (Regulation 47(a)) Within 30 working days of renewal. In any other case by 15 May 2013

2. Deposit received on or after 7 March 2011 and before 2 July 2012

By 13 November 2012

3. Deposit received on or after 2 July 2012 and before 2 October 2012

By 13 November 2012

4. Deposit received on or after 2 October 2012

Within 30 working days of the beginning of the tenancy

Information about the schemes

Further details about the individual schemes are available on the individual scheme web sites below. Email addresses and telephone numbers are also included. All three schemes have a range of information available for both landlords (and their agents) as well as tenants and these include how landlords can join the schemes, how to submit deposits, how to ask for repayment of deposits and how the dispute resolution service will work.

Letting Protection Service Scotland

www.lettingprotectionscotland.com

Address:

The Pavilions

Bridgwater Road

Bristol

BS99 6BN

Email contact: events@lettingprotectionscotland.com
Telephone: 0330 303 0031

SafeDeposits Scotland
www.safedepositsscotland.com
Address:
Lower Ground
250 West George Street
Glasgow
G2 4QY
Email contact: info@safedepositsscotland.com
Telephone: 03333 213 136

Mydeposits Scotland
www.mydepositsscotland.co.uk
Address:
Premiere House
Elstree Way
Borehamwood
Hertfordshire
WD6 1JH
Email contact: info@mydepositsscotland.co.uk
Telephone: 0333 321 9402

****

Chapter 14

Income Tax and Financial Management

Stamp Duty on a buy to let property

Stamp duty (or Stamp Duty Land Tax (SDLT) to give it its full name) is payable on a buy to let property. The amount varies depending on the price of the property.

The current rates of stamp duty from 1st April 2016 for buy to let properties are;

- 3% tax on the first £125,000
- 5% on the portion up to £250,000
- 8% on the portion up to £925,000
- 13% on the portion up to £1.5 million
- 15% on everything over that

Anyone buying a second property that isn't their main residence will be charged these new rates. This will include holiday lets and buying a property for children if the parents leave their name on the title deeds. Stamp duty has to be paid within 30 days of completion of the purchase of the property although this is usually paid by the solicitor on completion. The amount of Stamp Duty paid is deductible from any capital gains you might make when the property is sold.

Capital Gains Tax (CGT) on buy to let property

If you sell the property for more than you paid for it after deducting costs such as stamp duty and estate agent/solicitors fees you will be liable for CGT. By making a profit, you are essentially 'gaining capital', and so the tax applies. However, as an individual you get an annual allowance to set against any gain.

In the 2017/2018 tax year, this allowance is £11,300. This is a special allowance purely for capital items and is separate from the annual personal income tax allowance. If the gain is greater than the £11,300 allowance, you will pay tax at a rate of either 18% or 28% on that profit depending on the amount of income and capital gains you have.

Note that the lower CGT rates of 10% and 20% announced in the March 2016 budget do not apply to landlords and buy to let properties.

Reducing CGT liability

There are legitimate ways to reduce the amount of Capital Gains Tax (CGT) payable:

• A loss made on the sale of a buy to let property in previous years
• Solicitor fees
• Estate agent fees
• Costs of advertising the property for sale
• Stamp duty
• Any expenditure on 'capital' items

These expenses can be deducted from your capital gain. There are also certain tax reliefs available. For example if the property was previously your main residence, the gain may be reduced.

Like income tax, any gain is declared on your Self Assessment tax return. The tax is therefore payable by the 31st January in the year after the tax year in which the property was sold. (E.g. if a property was sold on 4th May 2015 it is in the tax year to 5th April 2016 so the tax is payable by 31st January 2017.) However, from April 2019, any tax payable on the profit of the sale of the property will be payable within 30 days of the date the property is sold.

Tax on buy to let property income

The income you receive as rent is taxable. You need to declare any rent you receive as part of your Self Assessment tax return. The tax on your income is then charged in accordance with your income tax banding (20% for basic rate taxpayers, 40% for higher rate, and 45% for additional rate). However, you can minimise the tax you have to pay by deducting certain 'allowable expenses' from your taxable rental income. Allowable expenses include:

• Interest on buy to let mortgages and other finance charges (but see below)
• Council tax, insurance, ground rents etc
• Property repairs and maintenance – however large improvements such as extensions etc will not be income tax deductible. They will be added

to the cost of the property when it is sold and be deductible against any capital gain.

• Legal, management and other professional fees such as letting agency fees.

• Other property expenses including buildings insurance premiums

The 2015 Summer Budget has reduced the amount of tax relief that is available for interest on buy to let mortgages from April 2017.

Prior to April 2017, tax is payable on your net rental income after deducting allowable expenses including mortgage interest. This meant that landlords paying higher (40%) or additional (45%) rate tax could claim tax relief at their highest rate.

However, from April 2020 tax relief can only be reclaimed at the basic rate (20%), whatever rate of tax the landlord pays. The rules are being phased in over 4 years commencing April 2017.

Worked example of interest deduction new rules

• House is bought for £300,000
• 80% mortgage is taken for £240,000
• Mortgage interest assumed at 4.5% annual mortgage interest is £10,800
• Rental yield is assumed at 5%, annual rent is £15,000

Basic rate taxpayer (see overleaf)

	2016/17	2017/18	2018/19	2019/20	2020 on
Annual rental income	£15,000	£15,000	£15,000	£15,000	£15,000
Mortgage interest payable	(£10,800)	(£10,800)	(£10,800)	(£10,800)	(£10,800)
Reduction in mortgage interest allowance*		£2,700	£5,400	£8,100	£10,800
Total rental income on which tax is payable	£4,200	£6,900	£9,600	£12,300	£15,000
Tax at 20%	£840	£1,380	£1,920	£2,460	£3,000
Tax relief at basic rate - 20% of the reduction in mortgage interest allowance		(£540)	(£1,080)	(£1,620)	(£2,160)
Total tax payable	£840	£840	£840	£840	£840

A basic rate tax payer on the face of it will not pay any more tax under the new rules, but that's not the whole story.

The new rules change the way income is calculated. Income is now before deduction of any mortgage interest. In the above example, in 2016-17 (before the new rules), your income was £4,200. In 2020 your income is deemed to be £15,000.

For example, if a person has £35,000 of employment income and rental income of £15,000 and mortgage interest is £10,800.

• Under the old rules the net profit of £4,200 and £35,000 employment income would all be taxed at the lower rate of 20%.
• Under the new rules, from 2020, the income from rental of £15,000

and employment income of £35,000 would even after the personal allowance take the taxpayer into the higher rate tax bracket of 40%. (currently income greater then £42,385). This increase in income could also affect claims for Child Benefit and Income Tax Credits.

The reduction in mortgage interest allowance is 0% in 2016-17, 25% in 2017-18, 50% in 2018-19, 75% in 2019-20, 100% in 2020 and beyond.

Higher rate taxpayer

The tax impact of the new interest deduction rules will be a significant increase to the tax bill for higher rate taxpayers. In 2020, a higher rate tax payer would pay £2,160 more tax.

	2016/17	2017/18	2018/19	2019/20	2020 on
Annual rental income	£15,000	£15,000	£15,000	£15,000	£15,000
Mortgage interest payable	(£10,800)	(£10,800)	(£10,800)	(£10,800)	(£10,800)
Reduction in mortgage interest allowance*		£2,700	£5,400	£8,100	£10,800
Total rental income on which tax is payable	£4,200	£6,900	£9,600	£12,300	£15,000
Tax at 40%	£1,680	£2,760	£3,840	£4,920	£6,000
Tax relief at basic rate - 20% of the reduction in mortgage interest allowance		(£540)	(£1,080)	(£1,620)	(£2,160)
Total tax payable	£1,680	£2,200	£2,760	£3,300	£3,840

*The reduction in mortgage interest allowance is 0% in 2016-17, 25% in 2017-18, 50% in 2018-19, 75% in 2019-20, 100% in 2020 and beyond

Using a limited company to minimise tax

There is no simple answer to this. It depends on a number of factors such as how many properties you hold, whether you need the income quickly and how long you want to hold the properties for and your individual circumstances.

Limited companies are not affected by the new Mortgage interest relief restriction coming in from April 2017. Interest for limited companies is classed as a business expense and fully deductible against income.

Companies pay corporation tax at a fixed rate irrespective of the size of the profits. The Corporation Tax rate is currently at 20% reducing to 17% in 2020. This makes the tax rate very attractive compared to 40% for higher rate tax payers and 45% for additional higher rate taxpayers.

The question is how the money in the company is passed to the individual. If the money is taken out of the company as a dividend, then from April 2016 only the first £5,000 of dividend income is tax free. Any dividends taken out in excess of this will either be charged at 7.5% for a basic rate taxpayer 32.5% for a higher rate taxpayer or 38.1% for an additional higher rate taxpayer. This tax is after the corporation tax at 20% has been paid.

116

The money could be taken as a salary, however the company would have to operate PAYE and pay Employers National insurance contributions on any salaries paid. This usually in most circumstances works out more expensive than paying dividends.

Companies do also not benefit from the annual allowance of £11,100 against capital gains. So extracting the money for a sold buy to let property could be less tax efficient than holding the property as an individual.

As you have to pay the 20% corporation tax on any gain, no annual allowance is given and you have to pay tax on extracting the money from the company, whereas even a higher rate taxpayer only pays 28% on any gain from the sale of a buy to let as an individual. Companies also have to prepare accounts to be filed with company's house, prepare and file corporation tax returns which can be more onerous than self-assessment returns.

Interest rates charged on mortgages to companies have historically been higher than to individuals so further investigation of the comparison of the rates charged should be considered alongside the tax implications.

Transferring a current buy to let property into a limited company can trigger stamp duty and capital gains tax charges at the time of transfer so advice should be sought before undertaking such a transaction. Due to the complexities of this area it is essential that you seek proper professional advice.

Inheritance tax on a buy to let property

Inheritance Tax is payable on buy to let properties but the amount changes depending on your circumstances. A buy to let property that you own will form part of your estate for Inheritance Tax purposes.

It works like this:

If you're operating as a sole landlord – with the buy to let mortgage in your name as an individual and your estate entirely owned by you alone – then you're liable to inheritance tax if your property value less any outstanding mortgage (or combined value of your estate) exceeds £325,000.

If you're in this with a married or civil partner, then you each have a threshold of £325,000 so the inheritance tax kicks in at £650,000. Anything above these amounts is taxed at 40%. Inheritance tax planning is complex and definitely something that should be discussed with an expert tax or financial adviser.

****

Useful websites

The Buying Process-general

The Local Government Association

www.lga.gov.uk

Confederation of Scottish Local Authorities

www.cosla.gov.uk

Greater London Authority

www.london.gov.uk

The Environment Agency

www.environment-agency.gov.uk

www.homecheckuk.com

House Prices

Halifax www.halifax.co.uk

Nationwide www.nationwide.co.uk

Land Registry www.landreg.gov.uk

www.zoopla.co.uk

www.ourproperty.co.uk

Property Search Sites

www.hometrack.co.uk

www.rightmove.co.uk

www.zoopla.co.uk

www.findaproperty.com

www.primelocation.com

www.onthemarket.com

www.home.co.uk

findahood.com

propertynetwork.net

findproperly.co.uk

propertyauctionaction.co.uk

uniquepropertybulletin.co.uk

The buying and selling process-law and taxation

The Law Society www.lawsoc.org.uk

The Council of Mortgage Lenders www.cml.org.uk

HM Customs and Revenue www.hmrc.gov

Scotland

Law Society of Scotland www.scotlaw.org.uk

Leasehold/freehold

Lease www.lease-advice.org

Association of Residential Managing Agents

www.arma.org.uk

Mortgage search sites/brokers

Money facts www.moneyfacts.co.uk

www.moneysupermarket.co.uk

www.moneynet.co.uk

New homes
NHBC www.nhbc.co.uk

Renting and Letting
Association of Residential Letting Agencies (ARLA)

ARLA Administration

Maple House

53-55 Woodside Road

Amersham

Bucks

HP6 6AA

Tel: 01923 896555

Website: www.arla.co.uk

Email: info@arla.co.uk

Auctions
www.propwatch.com

www.primelocation.com

www.bbc.co.uk/homes/property/buying_auction

www.propertyauctions.com

www.netguide.co.uk/Buying_A_House_At_Auction

propertyauctionaction.co.uk

A SUMMARY OF IMPORTANT TERMS

FREEHOLDER: Someone who owns their property outright.

LEASEHOLDER: Someone who has been granted permission to live on someone else's land for a fixed term.

TENANCY: One form of lease, the most common types of which are fixed-term or periodic.

LANDLORD: A person who owns the property in which the tenant lives.

LICENCE: A licence is an agreement entered into whereby the landlord is merely giving you permission to occupy his/her property for a limited period of time.

TRESPASSER: Someone who has no right through an agreement to live in a property.

PROTECTED TENANT: In the main, subject to certain exclusions, someone whose tenancy began before 15th January 1989.

ASSURED TENANT: In the main, subject to certain exclusions, someone whose tenancy began after 15th January 1989.

NOTICE TO QUIT: A legal document giving the protected tenant twenty eight days notice that the landlord intends to apply for possession of the property to the County Court.

GROUND FOR POSSESSION: One of the stated reasons for which the landlord can apply for possession of the property.

MANDATORY GROUND: Where the judge must give possession of the property.

DISCRETIONARY GROUND: Where the judge may or may not give possession, depending on his own opinion.

STUDENT LETTING: A tenancy granted by a specified educational institution.

HOLIDAY LETTING: A dwelling used for holiday purposes only.

ASSURED SHORTHOLD TENANCY: A fixed-term post-1989 tenancy.

PAYMENT OF RENT: Where you pay a regular sum of money in return for permission to occupy a property or land for a specified period of time.

FAIR RENT: A rent set by the Rent Officer every two years for most pre-1989 tenancies and is lower than a market rent.

MARKET RENT: A rent deemed to be comparable with other non-fair rents in the area.

RENT ASSESSMENT COMMITTEE: A committee set up to review rents set by either the Rent Officer or the landlord.

PREMIUM: A sum of money charged for permission to live in a property.

DEPOSIT: A sum of money held against the possibility of damage to property.

QUIET ENJOYMENT: The right to live peacefully in your own home.

REPAIRS: Work required to keep a property in good order.

IMPROVEMENTS: Alterations to a property.

LEGAL AID: Help with your legal costs, which is dependent on income.

HOUSING BENEFIT: Financial help with rent, which is dependent on income.

HOUSING ADVICE CENTRE: A center which exists to give advice on housing-related matters and which is usually local authority-funded.

124

LAW CENTRE: A center, which exists for the purpose of assisting the public with legal advice.

****

Index

****

Appendix 1

A landlord checklist of things to do before tenants move in

➢ Check tenants have the 'Right to Rent' Landlords must ensure tenants can legally reside in the UK before letting to them. The penalty for renting to someone without the right to rent is a £3,000 fine or even imprisonment. The government has issued a list of commonly available documents to check. If your tenants have the right to rent, take a copy of the document and keep it on file.

➢ Protect the deposit. Deposit protection is a legal requirement for landlords. Landlords must protect deposits within 30 days of receiving funds, or face a fine of up to three times the deposit amount.

➢ Make your property fire safe A smoke alarm must be on all floors of the property, and carbon monoxide detectors must be in any rooms with fuel-burning devices. If your property comes with furniture, it should be flame resistant.

➢ Make sure your Gas Safety Certificate is up to date If there's a gas supply at the property, you must arrange a gas safety inspection each year. You must give a copy of the certificate to tenants at the start of a tenancy.

➢ Make sure your EPC is up to date Landlords must have a valid EPC (Energy Performance Certificate) to let a property legally in the UK. You must give a copy of the certificate to tenants at the start of a tenancy.

➤ Give tenants a copy of the 'How to Rent' guide This guide lists landlord obligations and tenants' rights. You must either give tenants a hard copy or email it to them as an attachment. A link to the guide is not enough. Landlords who fail to do this are unable to evict tenants under a Section 21 Notice.

➤ Make sure appliances are in working order Any appliance left in the property must be safe to use. Anything not working should be replaced or removed.

You should also:

➤ Reference your tenants This is the best insight into your tenant's ability to pay their rent on time. A good referencing service will check affordability, employability, credit history, and a previous landlord reference.

➤ Prepare an inventory Although not a legal requirement, an inventory is vital for getting funds from the deposit. If tenants disagree with your deductions, you won't be able to claim anything without a signed inventory.

➤ Take meter readings This keeps things fair. It means tenants will know what they're responsible to pay, and helps prevent landlords from being left with outstanding payments.

➤ Update utility suppliers It's a good idea to update utility suppliers with new tenant details. This ensures any utilities tenants use will be billed to them.

➤ Provide emergency contact numbers Important — especially for minimising any damage caused to the property. If a pipe bursts in the middle of the night, for example, your tenants need to know who to call.

➤ Change the locks Some might view this as an additional expense, but it could be essential for the safety of your new tenants. If you don't change the locks, you must be confident your previous tenants were trustworthy enough to return all copies of the keys.

****

Appendix 2

Sample Assured Shorthold Tenancy Agreement (England and Wales) with inventory

Sample Notice Requiring possession S6

Sample tenancy Scotland

Sample Notices Scotland

ASSURED SHORTHOLD TENANCY AGREEMENT ENGLAND AND WALES

This Tenancy Agreement is between

Name and address of Landlord-
-AND

Name of tenant:

Tenant"

(in the case of Joint Tenants the term "Tenant" applies to each of them and the names of all Joint Tenants should be written above. Each Tenant individually has the full responsibilities and rights set out in this Agreement)

Address-in respect of:

("the Premises")

Description of Premises
-Which comprises of:
Term-The Tenancy is granted for a fixed term of [6] months

Date of start of tenancy-The Tenancy begins on:

("The Commencement Date") and is an assured shorthold monthly tenancy, the terms of which are set out in this Agreement.

Overcrowding-The Tenant agrees not to allow any person other than the Tenant to reside at the Premises.

Payment of Deposit-The Tenant agrees to pay on signing the Agreement a deposit of £   which will be returnable in full providing that the Landlord may deduct from such sums: The reasonable costs of any necessary repairs to the premises, building or common parts, or the replacement of any or all of the contents where such repair or replacement is due to any act or omission of the Tenant or family or visitors of the Tenant, such sums as are outstanding on leaving the Premises in respect of arrears or other charges including Court costs or other fees.

The deposit will be protected by The Deposit Protection Service (The DPS) in accordance with the Terms and Conditions of The DPS. The Terms and Conditions and ADR Rules governing the protection of the deposit including the repayment process can be found at www.depositprotection.com

Payment for the premises-
Rent: The rent for the premises is:

Service Charge:
Total:

In this Agreement the term "Rent" refers to the net rent and service charge set out above or as varied from time to time in accordance with this Agreement. The payment of monthly Rent is due in advance on the first Saturday of each month.

The service charge is in respect of the landlord providing the services listed in Schedule 1 to this Agreement for which the Tenant shall pay a service charge to be included in the rent. The service charge may be varied by the landlord in accordance with the terms set out in Schedule 1 to this Agreement.

I/We have read, understood and accept the terms and conditions contained within this agreement which include the standard terms and conditions attached.

Signed by the Tenant

.... Dated:

Signed on behalf of the landlord

.... Dated:

If the Tenant feels that the landlord has broken this Agreement or not performed any obligation contained in it, he/she should first complain to the landlord in writing giving details of the breach or non-performance.

Terms and Conditions

1. It is agreed that:
Changes in Rent-1.1-The landlord may increase or decrease the Rent

by giving the Tenant not less than 4 weeks notice in writing of the increase or decrease. The notice shall specify the Rent proposed. The first increase or decrease shall be on the first day of   following the Commencement Date of this Agreement. Subsequent increases or decreases in the Rent shall take effect on the first day of   in each subsequent year. The revised Rent shall be the amount specified in the notice of increase unless the Tenant exercises his/her right to refer the notice to a Rent Assessment Committee to have a market rent determined in which case the maximum Rent payable for one year after the date specified in the notice shall be the Rent so determined.

Altering the Agreement-1.2-With the exception of any changes in Rent, this Agreement may only be altered by the agreement in writing of both the Tenant and the landlord.

2. The landlord agrees:

Possession-2.1-To give the Tenant possession of the Premises at the commencement of the Tenancy.

Tenant's Right to Occupy-2.2-Not to interrupt or interfere with the Tenant's right peacefully to occupy the Premises except where:
(i)   access is required to inspect the condition of the Premises or to carry out repairs or other works to the Premises or adjoining property; or
(ii)   a court has given the Association possession by ending the Tenancy.

Repair of Structure and Exterior-2.3-To keep in good repair the structure and exterior of the Premises including:

(i)   drains, gutters and external pipes;

(ii)   the roof;

(iii)   outside wall, outside doors, windowsills, window catches, sash cords and window frames including necessary external painting and decorating;

(iv)   internal walls, floors and ceilings, doors and door frames, door hinges and skirting boards but not including internal painting and decoration;

(v)   plasterwork;

(vi)   chimneys, chimney stacks and flues but not including sweeping;

(vii)   pathways, steps or other means of access;

(viii)   integral garages and stores;

(ix)   boundary walls and fences.

Repair of Installations-2.4-To keep in good repair and working order any installations provided by the landlord for space heating, water heating and sanitation and for the supply of water, gas and electricity including:

(i)   basins, sinks, baths, toilets, flushing systems and waste pipes;

(ii)   electric wiring including sockets and switches, gas pipes and water pipes;

(iii)   water heaters, fireplaces, fitted fires and central heating installations

Repair of Common Parts-2.5-To take reasonable care to keep the common entrances, halls, stairways, lifts, passageways, rubbish chutes and any other common parts, including their lighting, in reasonable repair and fit for use by the Tenant and other occupiers and visitors to the Premises.

External & Internal
Decorations-2.6-To keep the exterior and interior of the Premises and any common parts in a good state of decoration and normally to decorate these areas once every 5 years.

3. The Tenant agrees:

Possession-3.1-To take possession of the Premises at the commencement of the Tenancy and not to part with possession of the Premises or sub-let the whole or part of it.

Rent-3.2-To pay the Rent monthly and in advance. The first payment shall be made on the signing of the Agreement in respect of the period from the Commencement Date to the first Saturday of the following month.

Use of Premises-3.3-To use the Premises for residential purposes as the Tenant's only or principal home and not to operate a business at the Premises without the written consent of the landlord.

Nuisance and Racial and other Harassment-3.4-Not to behave or allow members of his/her household or any other person visiting the Premises with the Tenant's permission to behave in a manner nor do anything which is likely to be a nuisance to the tenants, owners or lessees of any of the other properties or other persons lawfully visiting the property. In particular, not to cause any interference, nuisance or annoyance through noise, anti-social behaviour or threats of or actual violence or any damage to property belonging to the said persons. This Clause also applies to any conduct or activity which amounts to harassment including: abuse and intimidation, creating unacceptable levels of noise or causing intentional damage or any other persistent behaviour which causes offence, discomfort or inconvenience on the grounds of colour, race religion, sex, sexual orientation and disability.

Noise-3.5-Not to play or allow to be played any radio, television, audio equipment or musical instrument so loudly that it causes a nuisance or annoyance to neighbours or can be heard outside the Premises.

Domestic Violence-3.6-Not to use or threaten violence against any other person living in the Premises such that they are forced to leave by reason of the Tenant's violence or fear of such violence.

Pets-3.7-To keep under control any animals at the Premises and to obtain the written consent of the landlord before keeping a dog or any other animal.

Car Repairs-3.8-That no car servicing or car repairs shall be carried out in the roads or accessway or parking spaces or in the forecourt or approaches to the Premises, such as to be a nuisance or annoyance to neighbours.

Paraffin-3.9-Not to use any paraffin or bottled gas heating, lighting or cooking appliances on the Premises nor any appliances which discharge the products of combustion into the interior of the Premises.

Vehicles-3.10-That no commercial vehicle, caravan, boat, or lorry shall be parked in the accessway or parking spaces (regardless of whether this forms part of the Premises) or in the forecourt or approaches to the Premises or the adjoining premises.

Keeping premises clean-3.11-To keep the interior of the Premises in a clean condition. The Tenant agrees to return the property in the same decorative order as at the start of the tenancy taking into account fair wear and tear.

Damage-3.12-To make good any damage caused wilfully or by neglect or carelessness on the part of the Tenant or any member of the Tenant's household or visitor to the Premises including the replacement of any broken glass in windows and repair or replacement of any damaged fittings and installations. If the Tenant fails to make good any damage for which he/she is responsible the landlord may enter the Premises and carry out the work in default and the cost of this work shall be recoverable by the Association from the Tenant.

Reporting Disrepair-3.13-To report to the landlord any disrepair or defect for which the landlord is responsible in the structure or exterior of the Premises or in any installation therein or in the common parts.

Access-3.14-To allow the landlords employees or contractors acting on behalf of the landlord access at all reasonable hours of the daytime to inspect the condition of the Premises or to carry out repairs or other works to the Premises or adjoining property. The landlord will normally give at least 24 hours' notice, but immediate access may be required and shall be given in an emergency.

Assignment-3.15-Not to assign the Tenancy.

Sub-Tenants-3.16-Not to sub-let the whole or part of the Premises.

Ending the Tenancy-3.17-To give the landlord at least [4] weeks notice in writing when the Tenant wishes to end the Tenancy.

Moving Out-3.18-To give the landlord vacant possession and return the keys of the Premises at the end of the Tenancy and to remove all personal possessions and rubbish and leave the Premises and the landlords furniture and fixtures in good lettable condition and repair. The landlord accepts no responsibility for anything left at the Premises by the Tenant at the end of the Tenancy.

4. The Tenant has the following rights:
Right to Occupy-4.1-The Tenant has the right to occupy the Premises without interruption or interference from the landlord for the duration of this Tenancy (except for the obligation contained in this Agreement to give access to the landlords employees or contractors) so long as the Tenant complies with the terms of this Agreement and has proper respect for the rights of other tenants and neighbours.

Security of Tenure-4.2-The Tenant has security of tenure as an assured tenant so long as he/she occupies the Premises as his/her only or principal home. Before the expiry of the fixed term the landlord can only end the Tenancy by obtaining a court order for possession of the Premises on one of the grounds listed in Schedule 2 of the Housing Act 1988. The landlord will only use the following grounds to obtain an order for possession

--The tenant has not paid rent which is due; (Ground 10)
The Tenant has broken, or failed to perform, any of the conditions of this Tenancy; (Ground 12)
The Tenant or anyone living in the premises has caused damage to, or failed to look after the premises, the building, any of the common parts; (Ground 13)
The Tenant or anyone living in the premises has caused serious or persistent nuisance or annoyance to neighbours, or has been responsible for any act of harassment on the grounds of race, colour, religion, sex, sexual orientation, or disability, or has been convicted of using the property for immoral or illegal purposes; (Ground 14) or because of domestic violence (Ground 14A)
Where the tenancy has devolved under the will or intestacy of the Tenant
Suitable alternative accommodation is available to the Tenant

Notice Periods for ending Assured Tenancy-4.3-Before the expiry of the fixed term the landlord agrees that it will not give less than four weeks notice in writing of its intention to seek a possession order except where it is seeking possession on Ground 14 or Ground 14A (whether or not combined with other Grounds) where it shall give such period of notice that it shall decide and that is not less than the statutory minimum notice period

Expiry of Tenancy-4.4-The landlord can only end the Tenancy by giving the Tenant at least two months notice that it requires possession of the Premises and, if the tenant does not vacate by the given date, by obtaining a court order for possession. The court will make an order for possession if it is satisfied that the proper notice has been given.

Cessation of Assured Tenancy-4.5-If the Tenancy ceases to be an assured tenancy the landlord may end the Tenancy by giving four weeks' notice in writing which shall be validly served on the Tenant if posted or delivered to the Premises.

****

ENGLAND, WALES AND SCOTLAND HOUSEHOLD INVENTORY

Re: (The Property)_____

Living room				
No	Item	Condition	In	Out
1	Armchair	Fair		(condition when leaving)
Etc Etc				
Kitchen				

Bathroom				
Hall				
Bedroom (1-2-3)				
Garden				
Other				

**Department for
Communities and
Local Government**

FORM 6A
Notice seeking possession of a property
let on an Assured Shorthold Tenancy

Housing Act 1988 section 21(1) and (4) as amended by section 194 and paragraph 103 of Schedule 11 to the Local Government and Housing Act 1989 and section 98(2) and (3) of the Housing Act 1996

Please write clearly in black ink. Please tick boxes where appropriate.

This form should be used where a no fault possession of accommodation let under an assured shorthold tenancy (AST) is sought under section 21(1) or (4) of the Housing Act 1988.

There are certain circumstances in which the law says that you cannot seek possession against your tenant using section 21 of the Housing Act 1988, in which case you should not use this form. These are:

(a) during the first four months of the tenancy (but where the tenancy is a replacement tenancy, the four month period is calculated by reference to the start of the original tenancy and not the start of the replacement tenancy – see section 21(4B) of the Housing Act 1988);

(b) where the landlord is prevented from retaliatory eviction under section 33 of the Deregulation Act 2015;

(c) where the landlord has not provided the tenant with an energy performance certificate, gas safety certificate or the Department for Communities and Local Government's publication "How to rent: the checklist for renting in England" (see the Assured Shorthold Tenancy Notices and Prescribed Requirements (England) Regulations 2015);

(d) where the landlord has not complied with the tenancy deposit protection legislation; or

(e) where a property requires a licence but is unlicensed.

Landlords who are unsure about whether they are affected by these provisions should seek specialist advice.

This form must be used for all ASTs created on or after 1 October 2015 except for statutory periodic tenancies which have come into being on or after 1 October 2015 at the end of fixed term ASTs created before 1 October 2015. There is no obligation to use this form in relation to ASTs created prior to 1 October 2015, however it may nevertheless be used for all ASTs.

What to do if this notice is served on you

You should read this notice very carefully. It explains that your landlord has started the process to regain possession of the property referred to in section 2 below.

You are entitled to at least two months' notice before being required to give up possession of the property. However, if your tenancy started on a periodic basis without any initial fixed term a longer notice period may be required depending on how often you are required to pay rent (for example, if you pay rent quarterly, you must be given at least three months' notice, or, if you have a periodic tenancy which is half yearly or annual, you must be given at least six months' notice (which is the maximum)). The date you are required to leave should be shown in section 2 below. After this date the landlord can apply to court for a possession order against you.

Where your tenancy is terminated before the end of a period of your tenancy (e.g. where you pay rent in advance on the first of each month and you are required to give up possession in the middle of the month), you may be entitled to repayment of rent from the landlord under section 21C of the Housing Act 1988.

If you need advice about this notice, and what you should do about it, take it immediately to a citizens' advice bureau, a housing advice centre, a law centre or a solicitor.

1. To:

   Name(s) of tenant(s) (Block Capitals)

   | |
   | |

2. You are required to leave the below address after [   ] [1]. If you do not leave, your landlord may apply to the court for an order under section 21(1) or (4) of the Housing Act 1988 requiring you to give up possession.

   Address of premises

   | |

---

1 Landlords should insert a calendar date here. The date should allow sufficient time to ensure that the notice is properly served on the tenant(s). This will depend on the method of service being used and landlords should check whether the tenancy agreement makes specific provision about service. Where landlords are seeking an order for possession on a periodic tenancy under section 21(4) of the Housing Act 1988, the notice period should also not be shorter than the period of the tenancy (up to a maximum of six months), e.g. where there is a quarterly periodic tenancy, the date should be three months from the date of service.

Form 6A

3. This notice is valid for six months only from the date of issue unless you have a periodic tenancy under which more than two months' notice is required (see notes accompanying this form) in which case this notice is valid for four months only from the date specified in section 2 above.

4. Name and address of landlord

To be signed and dated by the landlord or their agent (someone acting for them). If there are joint landlords each landlord or the agent should sign unless one signs on behalf of the rest with their agreement.

Signed

Date (DD/MM/YYYY)

Please specify whether: ☐ landlord ☐ joint landlords ☐ landlord's agent

Name(s) of signatory/signatories (Block Capitals)

Address(es) of signatory/signatories

Telephone of signatory/signatories

FORM 3

Notice seeking possession of a property let on an Assured Tenancy or an Assured Agricultural Occupancy

Housing Act 1988 section 8 as amended by section 151 of the Housing Act 1996, section 97 of the Anti-social Behaviour, Crime and Policing Act 2014, and section 41 of the Immigration Act 2016.

- Please write clearly in black ink.
- Please cross out text marked with an asterisk (*) that does not apply.
- This form should be used where possession of accommodation let under an assured tenancy, an assured agricultural occupancy or an assured shorthold tenancy is sought on one of the grounds in Schedule 2 to the Housing Act 1988.
- Do not use this form if possession is sought on the "shorthold" ground under section 21 of the Housing Act 1988 from an assured shorthold tenant where the fixed term has come to an end or, for assured shorthold tenancies with no fixed term which started on or after 28th February 1997, after six months has elapsed. Form 6A 'Notice seeking possession of a property let on an Assured Shorthold Tenancy' is prescribed for these cases.

1   To: ....

Name(s) of tenant(s)/licensee(s)*

2   Your landlord/licensor* intends to apply to the court for an order requiring you to give up possession of: ....
....
....
....

Address of premises

3   Your landlord/licensor* intends to seek possession on ground(s) .... in Schedule 2 to the Housing Act 1988 (as amended), which read(s): ....
....
....
....

Give the full text (as set out in the Housing Act 1988 (as amended) of each ground which is being relied on. Continue on a separate sheet if necessary.

4   Give a full explanation of why each ground is being relied on:...
....
....
....

Continue on a separate sheet if necessary.

Notes on the grounds for possession

- If the court is satisfied that any of grounds 1 to 8 is established, it must make an order (but see below in respect of fixed term tenancies).
- Before the court will grant an order on any of grounds 9 to 17, it must be satisfied that it is reasonable to require you to leave. This means that, if one of these grounds is set out in section 3, you will be able to suggest to the court that it is not reasonable that you should have to leave, even if you accept that the ground applies.
- The court will not make an order under grounds 1, 3 to 6[1], 9 or 16, to take effect during the fixed term of the tenancy (if there is one) and it will only make an order during the fixed term on grounds 2, 7, 7A, 8, 10 to 15 or 17 if the terms of the tenancy make provision for it to be brought to an end on any of these

---

[1] Amended to reflect changes shortly to be made to correct the form prescribed in the Assured Tenancies and Agricultural Occupancies (Forms) (England) Regulations 2015.

grounds. It may make an order for possession on ground 7B during a fixed-term of the tenancy even if the terms of the tenancy do not make provision for it to be brought to an end on this ground.

- Where the court makes an order for possession solely on ground 6 or 9, the landlord must pay your reasonable removal expenses.

5   The court proceedings will not begin until after: ....
....

Give the earliest date on which court proceedings can be brought

Notes on the earliest date on which court proceedings can be brought

- Where the landlord is seeking possession on grounds 1, 2, 5 to 7, 9 or 16 (without ground 7A or 14), court proceedings cannot begin earlier than 2 months from the date this notice is served on you and not before the date on which the tenancy (had it not been assured) could have been brought to an end by a notice to quit served at the same time as this notice. This applies even if one of grounds 3, 4, 7B, 8, 10 to 13, 14ZA, 14A, 15 or 17 is also specified.

- Where the landlord is seeking possession on grounds 3, 4, 7B, 8, 10 to 13, 14ZA, 14A, 15 or 17 (without ground 7A or 14), court proceedings cannot begin earlier than 2 weeks from the date this notice is served. If one of 1, 2, 5 to 7, 9 or 16 grounds is also specified court proceedings cannot begin earlier than two months from the date this notice is served.

- Where the landlord is seeking possession on ground 7A (with or without other grounds), court proceedings cannot begin earlier than 1 month from the date this notice is served on you and not before the date on which the tenancy (had it not been assured) could have been brought to an end by a notice to quit served at the same time as this notice. A notice seeking possession on ground 7A must be served on you within specified time periods which vary depending on which condition is relied upon:

  - Where the landlord proposes to rely on condition 1, 3 or 5: within 12 months of the conviction (or if the conviction is appealed: within 12 months of the conclusion of the appeal);

  - Where the landlord proposes to rely on condition 2: within 12 months of the court's finding that the injunction has been breached (or if the finding is appealed: within 12 months of the conclusion of the appeal);

  - Where the landlord proposes to rely on condition 4: within 3 months of the closure order (or if the order is appealed: within 3 months of the conclusion of the appeal).

- Where the landlord is seeking possession on ground 14 (with or without other grounds other than ground 7A), court proceedings cannot begin before the date this notice is served.

- Where the landlord is seeking possession on ground 14A, court proceedings cannot begin unless the landlord has served, or has taken all reasonable steps to serve, a copy of this notice on the partner who has left the property.

- After the date shown in section 5, court proceedings may be begun at once but not later than 12 months from the date on which this notice is served. After this time the notice will lapse and a new notice must be served before possession can be sought.

6   Name and address of landlord/licensor*.

To be signed and dated by the landlord or licensor or the landlord's or licensor's agent (someone acting for the landlord or licensor). If there are joint landlords each landlord or the agent must sign unless one signs on behalf of the rest with their agreement.

Signed .... *Date* ....
....
....

Please specify whether: landlord / licensor / joint landlords / landlord's agent

Name(s) (Block Capitals) ....
....

Address ....
....
....

Telephone: Daytime .... *Evening* ....

What to do if this notice is served on you

- This notice is the first step requiring you to give up possession of your home. You should read it very carefully.

- Your landlord cannot make you leave your home without an order for possession issued by a court. By issuing this notice your landlord is informing you that he intends to seek such an order. If you are willing to give up possession without a court order, you should tell the person who signed this notice as soon as possible and say when you are prepared to leave.

- Whichever grounds are set out in section 3 of this form, the court may allow any of the other grounds to be added at a later date. If this is done, you will be told about it so you can discuss the additional grounds at the court hearing as well as the grounds set out in section 3.

- If you need advice about this notice, and what you should do about it, take it immediately to a citizens' advice bureau, a housing advice centre, a law centre or a solicitor.

SHORT ASSURED TENANCY AGREEMENT

This is a Short Assured Tenancy within the meaning of section 32 of the Housing (Scotland) Act 1988

1. **PARTIES**

   THE LANDLORD IS:_____
   ("The Landlord")

   LANDLORD ADDRESS:_____

   _____

   _____

   LANDLORD TEL. NO:_____

   HMO 24 HOUR CONTACT NO. _____

   LANDLORD REGISTRATION NO. _ _ _ _ _ _ / _ _ _ / _ _ _ _ _

   THE TENANT IS/ARE:_____

   _____

   _____

   _____

   _____

   ("The Tenant (s)")

   Where this is a joint tenancy, the term "Tenant" applies to each of the individuals above and the full responsibilities and rights set out in this Agreement apply to each Tenant who will be jointly and severally liable.

2. **SUBJECTS**

   THE ACCOMMODATION LET IS:_____

   _____

   _____

   _____

   ("The Property address or identified room")

3. **COMMENCEMENT & DURATION:**

The tenancy will commence on _____ ("The start Date")

and will end on: _____ ("The end Date").

If the agreement is not brought to an end by either party on the end date, it will continue thereafter on a monthly basis until ended by either party.

4. **RENT AND OTHER CHARGES**

4.1 The rent is £_____ per calendar month payable monthly (in advance). The first payment will be paid at date of entry or before and subsequent payments are due and must be paid on or before the same date of each calendar month thereafter.

4.2 The Landlord may propose to increase the rent after the end date specified at Clause **3** above. Under such circumstances the Tenant will be given a minimum of 1 month's notice in writing of any proposed change before the beginning of the rental period when the change is to start.

5 **SERVICES**

The following services will be provided

(list the services together with the prices).

The Tenant hereby agrees to pay the service charges as required.

6 **DEPOSIT**

At the date of entry or before, a deposit of £ _____ will be paid by the Tenant to the Landlord or his agents. The Landlord or his agent will issue a receipt for the deposit to the Tenant. No interest shall be paid by the Landlord to the Tenant for the deposit.

6.1 The deposit will be paid into a tenancy deposit scheme within the timescales laid out in the **Tenancy Deposit Schemes (Scotland) Regulations 2011.**

6.2 The scheme administrator is _____

6.3 The Landlord will be entitled at the expiry or end of the lease to use the deposit to meet any outstanding sums or accounts due by the Tenant, the cost of repairing or replacing any of the fittings and fixtures which have been broken, damaged or lost and the expense of making good any failure by the Tenant to fulfil any of the other conditions of this lease.

6.4 The deposit or part of the deposit, if any, will be refunded to the Tenant within the timescales as laid out in the **Tenancy Deposit Schemes (Scotland) Regulations 2011**

7   **CONTENTS**

The Tenant agrees that the signed Inventory, attached as Schedule 1 to this Agreement is a full and accurate record of the contents of the accommodation at the start of the tenancy. The Tenant has a period of seven days after signing the Inventory to ensure that the Inventory is correct and to tell the Landlord of any discrepancies in writing, after which the Tenant shall be deemed to be fully satisfied with the terms.

7.1   The Tenant agrees that these contents were as described in the inventory. The Tenant agrees to replace or repair (or to pay the cost, at the option of the Landlord) any of the contents which are destroyed, damaged, removed or lost during the tenancy, fair wear and tear excepted. The costs involved in making good any damage or cleaning found necessary may be deducted by the Landlord from the deposit under Clause **6**

8   **LOCAL AUTHORITY TAXES**

The Tenant will be responsible for payment of the council tax and water and sewerage charges, or any local tax which may replace this. The Tenant will advise the local authority of the date of the start of the tenancy and the date of the end of the tenancy.

9   **HOUSEHOLD BILLS**

The Tenant undertakes to ensure that the accounts for the supply to the accommodation of gas, electricity and telephone are entered in his name with the relevant supplier. The Tenant agrees to pay promptly all sums that become due for these supplies relative to the period of the tenancy.

9.1   The Tenant agrees to make the necessary arrangements with the suppliers to settle all accounts for these services on termination of the tenancy. The Tenant agrees not to change supplier without the prior written permission of the Landlord. The Landlord may keep from the deposit any sum the Landlord expends or incurs in settling final accounts for the services at the end of the tenancy.

10   **INSURANCE**

The Landlord undertakes to pay all premiums for insurance of the building and contents belonging to him. The Landlord will have no liability for any items belonging to the Tenant. The Tenant is responsible for arranging insurance of his own belongings.

11   **OCCUPATION AND USE OF THE ACCOMMODATION**

11.1 ONLY OR PRINCIPAL HOME

The Tenant agrees to occupy the accommodation as his only or principal home and not to carry on any formal or registered trade business or profession there.

11.2 ABSENCES

The Tenant agrees to tell the Landlord if he is to be absent from the accommodation for any reason for a period of more than fourteen days. The Tenant agrees to take such measures to secure the accommodation prior to such absence as the Landlord may reasonably require and take appropriate measures to prevent frost or flood damage.

11.3 SUBLETTING & LODGERS

The Tenant agrees not to:
i.   assign this tenancy to any other person; or
ii.   sublet the accommodation in whole or in part; or
iii. take in lodgers or paying guests; or
iv.   allow other persons to share the occupation of the premises, whether or not for payment, without the prior written consent of the Landlord.

11.4 REASONABLE CARE

The Tenant agrees to take reasonable care of the accommodation and any common parts, and in particular agrees to take all reasonable steps to:
i.   keep the accommodation adequately ventilated and heated;
ii.   not bring any hazardous or combustible goods or material into the accommodation;
iii. not pour any oil, grease, or other damaging materials down the drains or waste pipes;
iv.   prevent water pipes freezing in cold weather;
v.   avoid danger to the accommodation or neighbouring properties by way of fire or flooding;
vi.   ensure the property and its fixtures and fittings are kept clean during the tenancy;
vii. not interfere with the smoke detectors, heat detectors or the fire alarm system;
viii. not interfere with door closer mechanisms.

11.5 ALTERATIONS

The Tenant agrees not to make any alteration to the accommodation, its fixtures or fittings, nor to carry out any internal or external decoration without the prior written consent of the Landlord.

Any request for adaptations, auxiliary aids or services as per the Equalities Act 2010 or the Housing (Scotland) Act 2006 must be made in writing to the Landlord. Consent for alterations requested under this legislation will not reasonably be withheld.

11.6 COMMON PARTS

In the case of flatted property the Tenant agrees, in conjunction with the other proprietors / occupiers, to sweep and clean the common stairway and to co-operate with other proprietors/properties in keeping the garden, back green or other communal areas clean and tidy.

Where a tenant fails in this responsibility, the Landlord may carry out these responsibilities and recover the costs from the Tenant.

11.7 ROOF

The Tenant is not permitted to access the roof.

11.8 REFUSE

The Tenant agrees to dispose of all rubbish in an appropriate manner and at the appropriate time. Rubbish must not be placed anywhere in the common stair at any time. The Tenant must take reasonable care to ensure that the rubbish is properly bagged. If rubbish is normally collected from the street it should not be put out earlier than 7am on the day of collection. Rubbish containers should be returned to their normal storage places as soon as possible after the rubbish has been collected. The Tenant must comply with any local arrangements for the disposal of large items (such as large electrical items).

11.9 STORAGE

Nothing belonging to the Tenant or anyone living with the Tenant or the visitors may be left or stored in the common stair if it causes nuisance or annoyance to neighbours.

11.10 DANGEROUS SUBSTANCES

The Tenant must not store keep on or bring into the premises or any store, shed or garage, inflammable liquids or explosive gasses which might reasonably be considered to be a fire hazard or otherwise dangerous to the premises or its occupants or the neighbours or the neighbour's property.

12   RESPECT FOR OTHERS

12.1   The Tenant, those living with him/her, and his/her visitors must not harass or act in an antisocial manner to, or pursue a course of antisocial conduct against any person in the neighbourhood. Such people include residents, visitors, agents and contractors and those in the Tenant's house.

12.2   "Antisocial" means causing or likely to cause alarm, distress, nuisance or annoyance to any person or causing damage to anyone's property. Harassment of a person includes causing the person alarm or distress. Antisocial conduct includes speech.
A course of conduct means antisocial behaviour on at least two occasions.

12.3   In particular, the Tenant, those living with him/her, and his/her visitors must not:

    i.   make excessive noise. This includes, but is not limited to, the use of televisions, hi-fis, radios and musical instruments and DIY tools;

    ii.   fail to control pets properly or allow them to foul or cause damage to other people's property;

    iii.   allow visitors to the Tenant's house to be noisy or disruptive;

    iv.   use the Tenant's house or allow it to be used, for illegal or immoral purposes;

    v.   vandalise or damage the Landlord's property or any part of the common parts or neighbourhood;

    vi.   leave rubbish ether in unauthorised places or at inappropriate times;

    vii. allow his/her children to cause nuisance or annoyance to other people by failing to exercise reasonable control over them;

   viii. harass, threaten or assault any other Tenant, member of his/her household, visitors, neighbours, members or employees of the Landlord or any other person or persons in the house, or neighbourhood, for whatever reason. This includes behaviour due to that person's race colour or ethnic origin, nationality, gender, sexuality, disability, age, religion or other belief, or other status;

    ix.   use or carry offensive weapons;

    x.   use or sell unlawful drugs or sell alcohol;

    xi.   store or bring onto the premises any type of firearm or firearm ammunition including any replica or decommissioned firearms.

The particular prohibitions on behaviour listed above do not in any way restrict the general responsibilities of the Tenant .

13.   PETS

The Tenant agrees not to keep any animals or pets in the accommodation without the prior written consent of the Landlord. Any such consent will not be unreasonably withheld.   Any pet (where permitted) will be kept under supervision and control to ensure that it does not cause deterioration in the accommodation, deterioration in the condition of common areas, nuisance either to neighbours or in the locality of the property.

14.   ACCESS

14.1 ROUTINE ACCESS

The Tenant agrees to give the Landlord access to the accommodation for the purpose of carrying out maintenance, repair or inspection, providing that written notice has been given to the Tenant no later than 24 hours beforehand that such access is required.

14.2 EMERGENCY ACCESS

The Tenant agrees to give Immediate access to the Landlord in an emergency whether or not notice has been given. The Landlord reserves the right to effect forcible entry to the accommodation should such access not be made available.

14.3 KEYS

The tenant has been given a key agreement that sets out the circumstances for the retention and use of keys by the landlord.

15   REPAIRS AND MAINTENANCE

15.1 THE REPAIRING STANDARD

The Landlord must ensure that the accommodation meets the Repairing Standard at the start of the tenancy and at all times during the tenancy. During the tenancy this duty applies only when the Tenant informs the

Landlord of work required or the Landlord becomes aware of it in some other way (inspection visit).

The Repairing Standard does not cover work for which you, as the Tenant, are responsible due to your duty to use the house in a proper manner; nor does it cover the repair or maintenance of anything that you are entitled to remove from the house.

If you believe that the landlord has failed to ensure that the house meets the Repairing Standard at all times during the tenancy, you have the right to apply to the Private Rented Housing Panel (PRHP). The PRHP may reject the application; consider whether the case can be resolved by us (the Tenant and Landlord) ourselves (for example, by agreeing to mediation); or refer your application to a Private Rented Housing Committee (PRHC) for consideration. The PRHC has power to require a Landlord to carry out work necessary to meet the Repairing Standard.

15.2 HABITABILITY

The Landlord agrees throughout the period of the tenancy to maintain the accommodation in a wind and watertight condition and in all other respects reasonably fit for human habitation.

15.3 STRUCTURE & EXTERIOR

The Landlord undertakes (together with any other owners of common parts of the building in which the accommodation is situated, if appropriate) to keep in repair the structure and exterior of the accommodation including the following:

i.   drains, gutters and external pipes;

ii. roof;

iii. outside walls, doors, windowsills, window catches, sash cords, and window frames;

iv. internal walls, floors, ceilings, doors, door frames, internal stair cases and landings;

v.   chimneys, chimney stacks, and flues (including sweeping);

vi. pathways, steps or other means of access;

vii. plaster work;

viii boundary walls and fences.

15.4 GAS SAFETY

The Landlord must ensure that there is an annual Gas safety check on all pipework and appliances. The check must be carried out by a Gas Safe Registered installer. The Tenant must be given a copy of the Landlords gas safety certificate. The Landlord must keep certificates for at least two years. The Gas Safety (Installation and use) Regulations 1998 places duties on Tenants to report any defects with gas pipework or gas appliances that they are aware of to the Landlord or letting agent. Tenants are forbidden to use appliances that have been deemed unsafe by a gas contractor.

15.5 LIQUID PETROLEUM GAS (LPG)

The use or storage of LPG is not permitted in the property.

15.6 INSTALLATIONS

The Landlord will keep in repair and in proper working order the installations in the accommodation for the supply of water, gas, electricity, sanitation, space heating and water heating (with the exception of those installed by the Tenant or which the Tenant is entitled to remove) including the following:

i. basins, sinks, baths, toilets, and showers;
ii. gas or electric fires and central heating systems;
iii. electrical wiring;
iv. door entry systems;
v. cookers;
vi. extractor fans.
vii smoke alarms

15.7 DEFECTIVE FIXTURES AND FITTINGS

The Landlord will repair or replace any of the fixtures, fittings or furnishings, supplied by the Landlord in the accommodation, which become defective through usual wear and tear; and will do so within a reasonable period of time. Nothing contained in this Agreement makes the Landlord responsible for repairing damage caused wilfully or negligently by the Tenant, anyone living with the Tenant or an invited visitor to the property. Should the Landlord be required to carry out the work, the Tenant must pay the cost of the repair. The Tenant hereby agrees to pay the costs of repair. This paragraph does not apply to damage caused by fair, wear and tear or vandals (provided that the Tenant has reported the damage to the Police and to the Landlord as soon as the damage is discovered).

15.8 REPAIR TIMETABLE

The Tenant undertakes to immediately notify the Landlord (or any officer, agent or employee specified by the Landlord for that purpose) of the need for any repair or emergency. The Landlord undertakes to carry out necessary repairs within a reasonable period of time after having been notified of the need to do so.

15.9 PAYMENT FOR REPAIRS

The Tenant will be liable for the cost of repairs where the need for them is attributable to his fault or negligence, that of any person residing with him, or any guest of his. The Landlord may deduct such costs at the termination of the tenancy from the deposit under Clause **6**.

16. LEGISLATION

The Landlord undertakes to secure repossession only by lawful means and to comply with all relevant legislation affecting private sector residential tenancies, and, where applicable, all legislation relating to other activities carried on in the premises, such as the provision of care or support, or food preparation.

17. DATA PROTECTION

Landlords and letting agents may share details about the performance of obligations under this agreement by the Landlord and Tenant; past, present and future known addresses of the parties, with each other, with credit and reference providers for referencing purposes and rental decisions; with Utility and Water Companies, local authority Council Tax and Housing Benefit departments, Mortgage lenders, to help prevent dishonesty, for administrative and accounting purposes, or for occasional debt tracing and fraud prevention. Under the Data Protection Act 1998 you are entitled, on payment of a fee which will be no greater than that set by statute, to see a copy of personal information held about you and to have it amended if it is shown to be incorrect.

18. ENDING THE TENANCY

This Short Assured Tenancy may be ended by:-

18.1 The tenancy reaching its end date and the Landlord giving two month's prior written notice that possession of the house is required in terms of section 33 of the Housing (Scotland) Act 1988 at that end date.

18.2 By the Landlord serving on the Tenant a Notice to Quit. The Landlord may serve such notice either:

    i. To terminate the tenancy at its end date

    ii. To terminate the tenancy where the Tenant has broken or not performed any of the obligations under this agreement.

18.3 By the Tenant giving the Landlord one month's notice in writing to terminate the tenancy at its termination date.

18.4 By the Landlord giving the Tenant the required Notice in the prescribed format in terms of Section 19 of the Housing (Scotland) Act 1988 of their intention to commence proceedings and then subsequently obtaining an order for recovery of possession from the Sheriff Court on one or more of the following grounds set out in schedule 5 of the Housing (Scotland) Act 1988. These grounds are as follows:-

HOUSING (SCOTLAND) ACT 1988: SECTION 18 (6) AND SCHEDULE 5 PARTS I AND II

Grounds 1-8 set out in Part 1 below are mandatory grounds: that is, if they are established the Sheriff must grant an order for possession.

Grounds 9-17 set out in Part II below are discretionary grounds: that is, even if they are established, the Sheriff will grant an order for possession only if he believes it is reasonable to do so.

Ground 1

Not later than the beginning of the tenancy the Landlord (or, where there are joint Landlords, any of them) gave notice in writing to the Tenant that possession might be recovered on this Ground or the sheriff is of the opinion that it is reasonable to dispense with the requirement of notice and (in either case)-

(a) at any time before the beginning of the tenancy, the Landlord who is seeking possession or, in the case of joint Landlords seeking possession, at least one of them occupied the house as his only or principal home; or

(b) the Landlord who is seeking possession or, in the case of joint Landlords seeking possession, at least one of them requires the house as his or his spouse's only or principal home, and neither the Landlord (or, in the case of joint Landlords, any one of them) nor any other person who, as Landlord, derived title from the Landlord who gave the notice mentioned above acquired the Landlord's interest in the tenancy for value.

Ground 2

The house is subject to a heritable security granted before the creation of the tenancy and-

(a) as a result of a default by the debtor the creditor is entitled to sell the house and requires it for the purpose of disposing of it with vacant possession in exercise of that entitlement; and

(b) either notice was given in writing to the Tenant not later than the date of commencement of the tenancy that possession might be recovered on this Ground or the Sheriff is satisfied that it is reasonable to dispense with the requirement of notice.

Ground 3

The house is let under a tenancy for a specified period not exceeding eight months and-

(a) not later than the date of commencement of the tenancy the Landlord (or, where there are joint Landlords, any of them) gave notice in writing to the Tenant that possession might be recovered under this Ground; and

(b) the house was, at some time within the period of 12 months ending on that date, occupied under a right to occupy it for a holiday; and for the purposes of this Ground a tenancy shall be treated as being for a specified period-

(i) not exceeding eight months, if it is determinable at the option of the Landlord (other than in the event of an irritancy being incurred) before the expiration of eight months from the commencement of the period of the tenancy; and

(ii) exceeding eight months, if it confers on the Tenant an option for renewal of the tenancy for a period which, together with the original period, exceeds eight months, and it is not determinable as mentioned in paragraph (i) above.

Ground 4

Where the house is let under a tenancy for a specified period not exceeding 12 months and-

(a) not later than the date of commencement of the tenancy the Landlord (or, where there are joint Landlords, any of them) gave notice in writing to the Tenant that possession might be recovered on this Ground; and

(b)   at some time within the period of 12 months ending on that date the house was subject to such a tenancy as is referred to in paragraph 7(1) of Schedule 4 to this Act; and for the purposes of this Ground a tenancy shall be treated as being for a specified period-

(i)   not exceeding 12 months, if it is determinable at the option of the Landlord (other than in the event of an irritancy being incurred) before the expiration of 12 months from the commencement of the period of the tenancy; and

(ii)   exceeding 12 months, if it confers on the Tenant an option for renewal of the tenancy for a period which, together with the original period, exceeds 12 months, and it is not determinable as mentioned in paragraph (i) above.

Ground 5

The house is held for the purpose of being available for occupation by a minister or a full-time lay missionary of any religious denomination as a residence from which to perform the duties of his office and-

(a)   not later than the beginning of the tenancy the Landlord (or, where there are joint Landlords, any of them) gave notice in writing to the Tenant that possession might be recovered on this ground; and

(b)   the sheriff is satisfied that the house is required for occupation by such a minister or missionary as such a residence.

Ground 6

The Landlord who is seeking possession or, where the immediate Landlord is a registered housing association within the meaning of the [1985 c. 69.] Housing Associations Act 1985, a superior Landlord intends to demolish or reconstruct the whole or a substantial part of the house or to carry out substantial works on the house or any part thereof or any building of which it forms part and the following conditions are fulfilled (and in those conditions the Landlord who is intending to carry out the demolition, reconstruction or substantial works is referred to as "the relevant Landlord")—

(a)   either-

(i)   the relevant Landlord (or, in the case of joint relevant Landlords, any one of them) acquired his interest in the house before the creation of the tenancy; or

(ii)   none of the following persons acquired his interest in the house for value—

(A)   the relevant Landlord (or, in the case of joint relevant Landlords, any one of them);

(B)   the immediate Landlord (or, in the case of joint immediate Landlords, any one of them), where he acquired his interest after the creation of the tenancy;

(C)   any person from whom the relevant Landlord (or any one of joint relevant Landlords) derives title and who acquired his interest in the house after the creation of the tenancy; and

(b)   the relevant Landlord cannot reasonably carry out the intended work without the Tenant giving up possession of the house because-

(i)   the work can otherwise be carried out only if the Tenant accepts a variation in the terms of the tenancy and the Tenant refuses to do so;

(ii)   the work can otherwise be carried out only if the Tenant accepts an assured tenancy of part of the house and the Tenant refuses to do so; or

(iii)   the work can otherwise be carried out only if the Tenant accepts either a variation in the terms of the tenancy or an assured tenancy of part of the house or both, and the Tenant refuses to do so; or

(iv)   the work cannot otherwise be carried out even if the Tenant accepts a variation in the terms of the tenancy or an assured tenancy of only part of the house or both.

Ground 7

The tenancy has devolved under the will or intestacy of the former Tenant and the proceedings for the recovery of possession are begun not later than twelve months after the death of the former Tenant or, if the sheriff so directs, after the date on which, in his opinion, the Landlord (or, where there are joint Landlords, any of them) became aware of the former Tenant's death. For the purposes of this Ground, the acceptance by the Landlord of rent from a new Tenant after the death of the former Tenant shall not be regarded as creating a new tenancy, unless the Landlord agrees in writing to a change (as compared with the tenancy before the death) in the amount of the rent, the period of the tenancy, the premises which are let or any other term of the tenancy.

Ground 8

Both at the date of the service of the notice under section 19 of this Act relating to the proceedings for possession and at the date of the hearing, at least three months rent lawfully due from the Tenant is in arrears.

Ground 9

Suitable alternative accommodation is available for the Tenant or will be available for him when the order for possession takes effect.

Ground 10

The following conditions are fulfilled-

(a)   the Tenant has given a notice to quit which has expired; and

(b)   the Tenant has remained in possession of the whole or any part of the house; and

(c)   proceedings for the recovery of possession have been begun not more than six months after the expiry of the notice to quit; and

(d)   the Tenant is not entitled to possession of the house by virtue of a new tenancy.

Ground 11

Whether or not any rent is in arrears on the date on which proceedings for possession are begun, the Tenant has persistently delayed paying rent, which has become lawfully due.

Ground 12

Some rent lawfully due from the Tenant-
- (a) is unpaid on the date on which the proceedings for possession are begun; and
- (b) except where subsection (1)(b) of section 19 of this Act applies, was in arrears at the date of the service of the notice under that section relating to those proceedings.

Ground 13

Any obligation of the tenancy (other than one related to the payment of rent) has been broken or not performed.

Ground 14

The condition of the house or of any of the common parts has deteriorated owing to acts of waste by, or the neglect or default of, the Tenant or any one of joint Tenants or any person residing or lodging with him or any sub-tenant of his; and, in the case of acts of waste by, or the neglect or default of, a person lodging with a Tenant or a sub-tenant of his, the Tenant has not, before the making of the order in question, taken such steps as he ought reasonably to have taken for the removal of the lodger or sub-tenant. In this Ground, "the common parts" means any part of a building containing the house and any other premises, which the Tenant is entitled under the terms of the tenancy to use in common with the occupiers of other houses.

Ground 15

The Tenant, a person residing or lodging in the house with the Tenant or a person visiting the house has-
- (a) been convicted of-
  - (i) using or allowing the house to be used for immoral or illegal purposes; or
  - (ii) an offence punishable by imprisonment committed in, or in the locality of, the house; or
- (b) acted in an antisocial manner in relation to a person residing, visiting or otherwise engaging in lawful activity in the locality; or
- (c) pursued a course of antisocial conduct in relation to such a person as is mentioned in head (b) above.

In this Ground "antisocial", in relation to an action or course of conduct, means causing or likely to cause alarm, distress, nuisance or annoyance, "conduct" includes speech and a course of conduct must involve conduct on at least two occasions and "Tenant" includes any one of joint Tenants."

Ground 16

The condition of any furniture provided for use under the tenancy has deteriorated owing to ill-treatment by the Tenant or any other person residing or lodging with him in the house and, in the case of ill-treatment by a person lodging with the Tenant or by a sub-tenant of his, the Tenant has not taken such steps as he ought reasonably to have taken for the removal of the lodger or sub-tenant.

Ground 17

The house was let to the Tenant in consequence of his employment by the Landlord seeking possession or a previous Landlord under the tenancy and the Tenant has ceased to be in that employment.

19.   NOTICE & DECLARATIONS

In signing this Agreement and taking entry to the accommodation, the Tenant:

i.   acknowledges that he was served a Form AT5, before the creation of this tenancy, and that he understands this tenancy to be a Short Assured Tenancy within the meaning of section 32 of the Housing (Scotland) Act 1988;

ii.   confirms that he has made full and true disclosure of all information sought by the Landlord in connection with the granting of this tenancy

iii.   confirms that he has not knowingly or carelessly made any false or misleading statements (whether written or oral) which might affect the Landlord's decision to grant the tenancy.

20.   INTERPRETATION

Declaring for the purposes of this lease that words importing the masculine gender shall include the feminine; words importing the singular shall include the plural, and where there are two or more persons included in the expression "the Tenant" the obligations and conditions incumbent upon and expressed to be made by "the Tenant", including payment of the rent, shall be held to bind all such persons jointly and severally.

Tenant Signature 1	Witness Signature
Tenant Full Name (Block Capitals)	Witness Full Name (Block Capitals)
Tenant Address	Witness Address
Date: Time:	Date: Time:

Tenant Signature 2	Witness Signature
Tenant Full Name (Block Capitals)	Witness Full Name (Block Capitals)
Tenant Address	Witness Address
Date: Time:	Date: Time:

Tenant Signature 3	Witness Signature
Tenant Full Name (Block Capitals)	Witness Full Name (Block Capitals)
Tenant Address	Witness Address
Date: Time:	Date: Time:

Tenant Signature 4	Witness Signature
Tenant Full Name (Block Capitals)	Witness Full Name (Block Capitals)
Tenant Address	Witness Address
Date: Time:	Date: Time:

Tenant Signature 5	Witness Signature
Tenant Full Name (Block Capitals)	Witness Full Name (Block Capitals)
Tenant Address	Witness Address
Date: Time:	Date: Time:

Landlord Signature	Witness Signature
Landlord Full Name (Block Capitals)	Witness Full Name (Block Capitals)
Landlord Address	Witness Address
Date: Time:	Date: Time:

**HOUSING (SCOTLAND) ACT 1988
AS AMENDED BY PARAGRAPH 85 OF SCHEDULE 17
TO THE HOUSING ACT 1988**

**NOTICE UNDER SECTION 19 OF INTENTION
TO RAISE PROCEEDINGS FOR POSSESSION**

IMPORTANT: INFORMATION FOR TENANT(S)

This notice informs you as tenant that your landlord intends to apply to the Sheriff for an Order for possession of the house at the address in Part 1, which is currently occupied by you.

Part 1   To..
(name of tenant(s))

of..

....

....

....
(address of house)

NOTE 1 TO TENANT.

IF YOU ARE UNCERTAIN ABOUT WHAT THIS MEANS, OR IF YOU ARE IN DOUBT ABOUT ANYTHING IN IT, OR ABOUT ITS VALIDITY OR WHETHER IT IS FILLED IN PROPERLY YOU SHOULD IMMEDIATELY CONSULT A SOLICITOR OR AN ORGANISASTION WHICH GIVES ADVICE ON HOUSING MATTERS. YOU MAY ALSO FIND IT HELPFUL TO DISCUSS THIS NOTICE WITH YOUR LANDLORD.

Part 2   I/We [on behalf of]* your landlord(s)

....

(name of landlord(s))

of..

....

....

(address and telephone number of landlord(s))

inform you that I/we* intend to raise proceedings for possession of the house at the address in Part 1 above on the following ground/grounds* being a ground/grounds* for possession as set out in Schedule 5 to the Housing (Scotland) Act 1988.

....

....

....

(give the ground number(s) and fully state ground(s) as set out in Schedule 5 of the Housing (Scotland) Act 1988: continue on additional sheets of paper if required)

NOTE 2 TO TENANT

A FULL LIST OF THE 17 GROUNDS FOR POSSESSION IN SCHEDULE 5 TO THE HOUSING (SCOTLAND) ACT 1988 TOGETHER WITH INFORMATION ON YOUR RIGHTS AS TENANT IS GIVEN IN THE BOOKLET "ASSURED TENANCIES IN SCOTLAND – A GUIDE FOR LANDLORDS AND TENANTS". IT IS AVAILABLE FROM ANY OFFICE OF THE RENT ASSESSMENT COMMITTEE, CITIZENS ADVICE BUREAU, HOUSING ADVISORY CENTRE OR FROM THE RENT REGISTRATION SERVICE.

Part 3   I/We also inform you that I/we are seeking possession under the above ground / grounds* for the following reasons :-

....

....

....

....

(state particulars of how you believe the ground(s) have arisen: continue on additional sheets of paper if required)

*delete as appropriate

Part 4   Proceedings will not be raised before …………………… (date) (which is the earliest date at which proceedings can be raised under Section 19 of the Housing (Scotland) Act 1988).

Signed ……………………………………………………………………

(Landlord(s) or Landlord's Agent)

Date …………………………………..

*delete as appropriate

FORM AT5: FOR USE ONLY BY A LANDLORD

ASSURED TENANCIES   **AT5**

HOUSING (SCOTLAND) ACT 1988

NOTICE UNDER SECTION 32 TO BE
SERVED ON A PROSPECTIVE TENANT
OF A SHORT ASSURED TENANCY

IMPORTANT: INFORMATION FOR PROSPECTIVE TENANT(S)

This notice informs you as prospective tenant(s) that the tenancy being offered by the prospective landlord(s) is a short assured tenancy under Section 32 of the Housing (Scotland) Act 1988.

Please read this notice carefully.

Part 1   To ....
(name of prospective tenant(s))

NOTE 1 TO PROSPECTIVE TENANT.

TO BE VALID THIS NOTICE MUST BE SERVED BEFORE THE CREATION OF A TENANCY AGREEMENT. A SHORT ASSURED TENANCY WILL NOT EXIST IF A VALID NOTICE HAS NOT BEEN SERVED.

Part 2   I your prospective landlord(s)/I your prospective landlord's agent*

....
(name of landlord(s))

of ....

....

....
(address and telephone number of landlord(s))

give notice that the tenancy being offered to you of the house at

....

....

....
(address of house)

*delete as appropriate

to which this notice relates is to be a short assured tenancy in terms of Section 32 of the Housing (Scotland) Act 1988.

Signed ....
(landlord(s) or landlord's agent)

Date ....

NOTE 2 TO PROSPECTIVE TENANT.

A SHORT ASSURED TENANCY IS A SPECIAL FORM OF TENANCY. UNLESS IT FOLLOWS IMMEDIATELY AFTER ANOTHER SHORT ASSURED TENANCY OF THE SAME HOUSE, (WITH THE SAME TENANT). IT MUST BE FOR NOT LESS THAN 6 MONTHS.

NOTE 3 TO PROSPECTIVE TENANT.

A LANDLORD OF A SHORT ASSURED TENANCY HAS SPECIAL RIGHTS TO REPOSSESS THE HOUSE. IF THE LANDLORD TERMINATES THE TENANCY BY ISSUING A VALID NOTICE TO QUIT AND GIVES THE TENANT AT LEAST 2 MONTHS NOTICE (OR A LONGER PERIOD IF THE TENANCY AGREEMENT PROVIDES) OF HIS INTENTION TO REPOSSESS THE HOUSE THE COURT MUST GRANT THE LANDLORD AN ORDER ALLOWING HIM TO EVICT THE TENANT IF HE APPLIES FOR ONE AT THE END OF THE TENANCY PERIOD SET OUT IN THE TENANCY AGREEMENT.

Part 3   Address and telephone number of agents if appropriate:

of landlord(s) agent   of Tenant(s) agent

....

....

....

....

....

NOTE 4 TO PROSPECTIVE TENANT.

A TENANT OF A SHORT ASSURED TENANCY HAS A SPECIAL RIGHT TO APPLY TO THE FIRST-TIER TRIBUNAL HOUSING AND PROPERTY CHAMBER FOR A RENT DETERMINATION FOR THE TENANCY.

NOTE 5 TO PROSPECTIVE TENANT.

IF YOU AGREE TO TAKE UP THE TENANCY **AFTER** YOUR LANDLORD HAS SERVED THIS NOTICE ON YOU YOUR TENANCY WILL BE A SHORT ASSURED TENANCY. YOU SHOULD KEEP THIS NOTICE IN A SAFE PLACE ALONG WITH THE WRITTEN DOCUMENT SETTING OUT THE TERMS OF TENANCY WHICH YOUR LANDLORD MUST PROVIDE UNDER SECTION 30 OF THE HOUSING (SCOTLAND) ACT 1988 ONCE THE TERMS ARE AGREED.

NOTE 6 TO PROSPECTIVE TENANT.

IF YOU REQUIRE FURTHER GUIDANCE ON ASSURED AND SHORT ASSURED TENANCIES, CONSULT A SOLICITOR OR ANY ORGANISATION WHICH GIVES ADVICE ON HOUSING MATTERS.

SPECIAL NOTES FOR EXISTING TENANTS

1.   If you already have a regulated tenancy, other than a short tenancy, should you give it up and take a new tenancy in the same house or another house owned by the same landlord, that tenancy cannot be an assured tenancy or a short assured tenancy. Your tenancy will continue to be a regulated tenancy.

2.   If you have a short tenancy under the Tenants' Rights Etc. (Scotland) Act 1980 or the Rent (Scotland Act 1984) your landlord can offer you an assured tenancy or short assured tenancy of the same or another house on the expiry of your existing tenancy.

3.   If you are an existing tenant and are uncertain about accepting the proposed short assured tenancy you are strongly advised to consult a solicitor or any organisation which gives advice on housing matters.

ASSURED TENANCIES

HOUSING (SCOTLAND) ACT 1988

NOTES FOR LANDLORDS TO BE READ WITH NOTICE AT5.
THESE NOTES ARE FOR GUIDANCE ONLY AND ARE A DEFINITIVE
INTERPRETATION OF THE LAW

WHEN TO USE THIS NOTICE

1.   You should use this notice only when you wish to inform a prospective tenant or tenants that the tenancy being offered by you is a short assured tenancy under Section 32 of the Housing (Scotland) Act 1988.

2.   You must serve the notice on the prospective tenant or tenants before the creation of any tenancy agreement. If it is not served before the creation of the tenancy agreement the tenancy will not be a short assured tenancy.

ABOUT SHORT ASSURED TENANCIES

3.   A short assured tenancy is a special form of assured tenancy which in the first instance must be for not less than 6 months. It gives you special rights to repossess the house (see paragraph 4) and special rights for tenants to apply to the First-tier Tribunal Housing and Property Chamber for a rent determination (see paragraphs 5 and 6).

Repossession of the property

4.   As landlord, if you obtain a possession order from the Sheriff, you may repossess the house you are letting on the short assured tenancy. Before applying for a possession order you must:

      4.1   Issue a valid Notice to Quit to terminate the tenancy at its expiry date, and not offer your tenant another tenancy:

      4.2   Give your tenant notice of your intention to apply for the order. The notice must be for at least 2 months unless your tenancy agreement provides for a longer period. If you fulfil these 2 conditions the Sheriff must grant you the order.

Rent

5.   Unless a rent for the tenancy has already been determined by the First-tier Tribunal Housing and Property Chamber, a tenant of a short assured tenancy has a right to seek a rent determination from the First-tier Tribunal Housing and Property Chamber at any time during the tenancy. On receiving an application, the First-tier Tribunal Housing and Property Chamber will consider if it is appropriate to determine a market rent.

6.   The First-tier Tribunal Housing and Property Chamber will make a rent determination only if it considers there is a sufficient number of similar houses in the locality let on assured tenancies and the rent payable for the tenancy is significantly higher than the landlord might reasonably expect to charge having regard to rent levels for those tenancies. A rent determination made by the First-tier Tribunal Housing and Property Chamber will be the maximum payable for the tenancy from the date specified.

HOW TO USE THIS NOTICE

7.   Before you and your prospective tenant make a binding agreement to let a house, you should complete Parts 1, 2 and 3 of the Notice. The Notice should then be given or sent to the prospective tenant or tenants. The tenancy will be a short assured tenancy as long as you have fulfilled all your requirements. The tenant should keep the Notice with the written document setting out the terms of the tenancy which have been agreed, and which must be provided by a landlord under Section 30 of the Housing (Scotland) Act 1988. You are also advised to keep a copy of Notice AT5 for your own records.

FURTHER GUIDANCE

8.   If you are uncertain about the question of tenancy status or uncertain about how to complete this Notice, you should consult a solicitor or any organisation which gives advice on housing matters.